GLORY DAYS

Royal Blue

Colin Morris

Ian Allan
PUBLISHING

Front cover:
Don't blink! No 1398
(736 MDV) was the first of 14
Bristol MW6G coaches
delivered with Royal Blue
fleetnames in 1963, but which
were re-titled 'Western
National' or 'Southern
National' by the following July.
The 39-seat bodywork is of the
stepped-waistline pattern
designed and built by Eastern
Coach Works for fitting to
latterday MW coaches of the
Tilling group of companies.
Calton Phoenix collection

Back cover:
In the years 1954 to 1956
inclusive, Royal Blue had to
make do with its existing
coaches and those 'hired in'
from other operators — a
process continued thereafter.
Neighbouring Tilling
companies Hants & Dorset and
Wilts & Dorset were favoured
after Southern and Western
National. A couple of the latter
are at Victoria with No 2211
(VDV 774) of 1957. The
traditional roof pannier and
steps have now been replaced
by 'vista' roof-lights.
Colin Billington collection

Contents

First published 2000

ISBN 0 7110 2727 7

All rights reserved. No part of this book may be reproduced or transmitted in any
form or by any means, electronic or mechanical including photocopying,
recording or by any information storage and retrieval system, without permission
from the Publisher in writing.

© Colin Morris 2000

Published by Ian Allan Publishing

an imprint of Ian Allan Publishing Ltd, Terminal House, Shepperton, Surrey
TW17 8AS

Printed by Ian Allan Printing Ltd, Riverdene Business Park, Hersham, Surrey
KT12 4RG.

Code: 0009/B2

Title page:
Start Bay, Devon, forms the
glorious backdrop for this
Southern National publicity
photograph taken in late spring
1957, near Torcross — some
way beyond the coach's
declared terminus of Torquay.
Yet the picture sums up the
geographical advantages
enjoyed by the Royal Blue
network — no wonder so many
thousands of passengers
booked holidays by Royal
Blue. The vehicle, in original
livery, is Bristol LS6G
No 2213 (VDV 776).
Calton Phoenix collection

Introduction

It would be best to begin by making clear that it is the 'Royal Blue' founded by Thomas Elliott in Bournemouth which is having its 'Glory Days' recounted, because several other firms have employed this elegant name. Among them were: John Clark, whose horsebuses were taken over by the London General Omnibus Company; G. Fowler & Sons' Isle of Wight Motor Services of Cowes; the Llandudno Coaching & Carriage Company; A. Burnett & Sons' Southsea Royal Blue Parlour Coaches Ltd; Henry Russett & Sons' Royal Blue Garage of Bristol; and W. G. Harrison's Royal Blue of Clapton, near Crewkerne — although the latter was more of a cornflower blue. Nowadays, 'Royalblue' in joined-up, lower-case computerspeak is a listed software services company — and doing very nicely, too. It is none of those.

This book exists thanks to the generosity of Peter Delaney, who has granted me access to his detailed and, as yet, unpublished material on Thomas Elliott and Royal Blue. He has read my drafts and kept me on course in masterly fashion. Participating with him in a joint blitz upon previously overlooked records has been extraordinarily revelatory in several respects. Some 'facts' with which local and transport historians have long grown comfortable are, evidentially, incorrect. Others have been misinterpreted or embroidered over the years. I hope to have tucked in a few loose ends.

My other thanks go back a long way. Those consulted between 1957 and 1970 included S. C. Bullock, R. J. Crawley, Mrs John T. G. Elliott, John Henry, Eric L. Jones, R. Keevil, Douglas W. Morison, J. C. Ransom, Harry Rollings, W. Wallace and J. T. Wilson.

Rather more recently, I have benefited from introductions made by John Birks and Roger Davies. I am indebted to Michael Rourke, Traffic Manager of Western National and, later, Managing Director of Southern National, for hospitality and information relating to the final years of Royal Blue. My thanks also to La Marchese Elsie Nobili-Vitelleschi of Bournemouth, Sir Simon Codrington, Bart of Dodington, the staff of the Dorset County Museum, Dorchester, the staff of Newscom plc, Bournemouth, and to the Librarian and staff of Bournemouth Library at Lansdowne for access to their respective records of the horse-and-carriage days, and to Hugh Bannister of Park Gate in respect of more recent events. Helen and Colin Billington of Fifield have been both generous and patient in response to my numerous requests, and I have been privileged to have access to the Billington collection — and to that of Peter Delaney.

As they have on numerous occasions previously, Alan Lambert, Phil Davies and Andrew Waller have loaned precious photographs for inclusion in one of my essays.

Colin Morris
Heswall
May 2000

3

1. Love and Marriage

The Elliotts' Royal Blue was founded in 19th-century Bournemouth. A 16th-century map of Dorset shows the county's boundary with Hampshire running along the length of the Bourne, a small stream rising in the parish of Kinson and, in those days, trickling over the sand into the blue waters of Poole Bay. Later, that boundary was pushed a mile to the west, but the area remained largely uninhabited heath and woodland. As late as 1803, just the isolated 'Bourn House' was situated beside the western bank of 'Bourn Chine' (a Hampshire name for a coastal ravine), which was crossed by a wooden bridge where now stands Bournemouth Square. The road from Poole to Christchurch — via Iford Bridge — passed to the north of this house and, unless its residents or visitors wished to travel, there was nothing to interrupt the progress of 'The Independent' from Weymouth to London, 'The Emerald' to Southampton, or other stage and mail coaches passing along its gravel track. Boscombe ('gorse valley') did not exist as anything other than a geographical feature.

The growth of Bournemouth amid its sylvan 'evergreen valley' has been well chronicled elsewhere, but what has not been made clear is that, in the first half of the 19th century and until 1855, Bournemouth's West Cliff area was part of the Branksome Estate. Much larger than present-day Branksome, this estate was located on both sides of the road to Poole and reached the shoreline west of Broad (later Branksome) Chine and the sea cliffs between Sugarloaf (later Branksome Dean) Chine and Durley Chine. It extended from Parkstone up to and including all that land west of the Bourne Stream and the estuary where now stands Bournemouth Pier. The name became extremely popular and at one stage, the estate's eastern end was called the 'Branksome Ward' of emergent Bournemouth. Its significance will emerge in the text.

Railways came bit by bit and comparatively late to the area. The line from Southampton to Dorchester, opened in June 1847, missed it completely, considering Ringwood and Wimborne far more important. A branch line to Hamworthy (Poole) was the closest it came — and it was left to Francis Butler to run a small omnibus twice a day from there to the Bath Hotel, Bournemouth. From the other direction, in 1851, William Humby, the proprietor of the King's Arms, Christchurch, began to collect passengers from Christchurch Road station (later called

Holmsley) in his small omnibus and run through to the Bath Hotel from the east, thus pioneering this much-lauded route.

When a branch railway line from Ringwood to Christchurch came into operation in November 1862, omnibuses and carriages run by several operators commenced thence to Bournemouth, although Humby, Francis Graham (the grandfather of the founder of Hants & Dorset Motor Services Ltd) and others continued to ply through to Holmsley at this time.

Meanwhile, Bournemouth turned up its nose at anything vulgar, and began to attract visits from European royalty. The Exeter Hotel on the West Cliff and the Bath on the East took on the prefix 'Royal'. Their patronage extended to the line of locally-owned carriages — and what had been built as the 'Branksome Stables' in Norwich Road became 'The Royal Branksome Mews' occupied under lease by William Coates. He reduced that title to a simple 'Royal Mews' so that it could fit over the entrance archway.

The largest 19th-century carriage undertaking in the resort was, however, that of Henry Laidlaw. He started in 1858 at Dalkeith Mews (and House) in Old Christchurch Road, not too far from The Square, as a 'riding and posting-master' — in other words, he provided post horses for the Royal Mail coaches which came that way. The gradual encroachment of the railways reduced that role and turned Laidlaw's into 'jobmasters, bus and carriage proprietors'.

During 1857, meanwhile, in faraway London, was born Thomas, the son of William Elliott, a Stepney grocer. His shop was just off Commercial Road, the eastern extension of which is the East India Dock Road. It is surely no coincidence that along this road at this time ran the 'Royal Blue' horsebus service which John Clark operated between Pimlico and Blackwall. That fleetname, on its dark blue background, could well have provided young Tom's first practical reading lessons as it was trundled impressively past his street some 24 times per day. Wide-eyed, he probably rode in Royal Blue buses — his introduction to travel.

Sadly, young Thomas Elliott's father died in 1863 and, I suspect so that he might benefit from the resinous perfume of the pines for which the town had now become famous, his mother elected to send him to live in Bournemouth with his uncle, a

◄◄ At Bournemouth Pier, c1890, three landaus and a double chair are on the stand whilst another double chair waits in its proper position on the West Wing. As a protection against the sun, blankets cover a horse and passenger seats, whilst a driver wears a pith helmet. One of these carriages probably belonged to Thomas Elliott. Licences for these vehicles were granted by Bournemouth's 'Horse Committee'.
Bournemouth Libraries/ Local History Collection

Inset:
Thomas Elliott, 1857-1911: Founded Branksome Mews in Avenue Lane, Bournemouth in October 1887, thereafter using the fleetname 'Royal Blue'. His great courtesy and attention to detail saw him established as the visitors' favourite proprietor of carriages — and provided the springboard for his sons to develop Royal Blue Automobile Services.
Colin Morris collection

This historic building, opened as 'Branksome Stables', was occupied by William Coates, one of the first jobmasters in Bournemouth. The title was altered to 'Royal Branksome Mews' — and then, just 'Royal Mews', so that the name would fit over the entrance. During the second half of the 19th century it was the base for Henry Laidlaw & Co's horse-drawn carriages. In the early 20th century, Elliott Bros occupied part of the building; it later became the registered office of Hants & Dorset Motor Services Ltd.
Charles Dunning / Colin Morris collection

This two-horse wagonette, probably Licence No 73, is believed to be the setting for an Elliott family photograph, with Thomas Elliott (in a boater, sitting on the footboard), Elizabeth Elliott (on the front seat) and sons Ted (with Royal Blue sash), Jack (centre) and Harry (in cap). The picture was taken c1902. A wagonette had bench seats facing inward.
Peter Delaney collection

local fishmonger. George Cutler lived and plied his trade at 7 Commercial Road, to the west of what became Bournemouth Square. Beside being a fish pedlar, Cutler set up as a small-carriage proprietor, commencing with bath chairs at The Pier (built in 1860). By 1877, he possessed two, pulled by pony but led on foot by the 'licensed driver'; by 1880 there were three,

plus a 'double chair' (a small four-wheeler with two seats plus another for the driver). He may well have hired out other small carriages — for which he would not have required licences. A brougham and a landau joined this fleet, which was possibly housed behind his premises, in nearby Avenue Lane.

Thomas Elliott was doubtless involved with his uncle's new enterprise, but it was not until September 1880 that the Horse Committee of the Bournemouth Improvement Commissioners — set up by Royal Assent on 14 July 1856 — granted him his first hackney-carriage driver's licence (No 217). He may well have driven passengers from the Royal Bath Hotel to Holmsley railway station that year, but documentary evidence strongly suggests it was not in his own vehicle; most likely it was in his uncle's landau. Indeed, when Thomas married Elizabeth Girvan in 1882, he gave his profession as 'cab driver', rather than 'proprietor'. It was not until 8 October 1885 that Thomas Elliott's own first vehicle — also a landau — was licensed by the committee (No 380) in his name. At first, the newly-weds lived in Ashley Road, Boscombe. Elizabeth loved her husband dearly, and would take a very active role in his forthcoming enterprise.

George Cutler died on 22 August 1886, and for a few months one of his sons was granted the licences and ran his carriages until their dispersal. One, a double-chair, became Thomas Elliott's property in April 1887 and, soon thereafter, he acquired a barouche (with seats for four passengers and one beside the driver). A site in Avenue Lane seems the likely location for their safe-keeping, together with his original landau.

Mr and Mrs Elliott now obtained the lease of land on the south side of Avenue Road, backing on to the end of Avenue Lane; building and moving into what they named 'Branksome Mews', next-door-but-one to an existing house called 'Branksome Lodge'. This must have irked Henry Laidlaw somewhat, because his firm had only recently dropped the word 'Branksome' from his 'Royal Branksome Mews', a property he had leased from John Cassels — together with William Coates' stock in trade — some 10 years earlier. Laidlaw had moved there from Dalkeith House together with his family, and by 1880 was calling this Norwich Road property simply 'Branksome Mews'. By 1889, a total of 32 licences was held by Laidlaw. In comparison, at that time Elliott held only seven for hackney carriages, which were housed at his version of 'Branksome Mews' in Avenue Road.

Under the circumstances, it was probably George Ames — another local jobmaster, and also the proprietor of the Oxford Riding School in Oxford Road, Bournemouth — rather than Laidlaw (who offered similar facilities), who taught Elliott how to drive 'four in hand', with four horses pulling the carriage and reins of each in the hands of the driver, without the aid of a postillion riding one of the leaders; this was considered the ultimate carriage-driving skill.

Thomas Elliott's brake No 23 amid the bracken in the depths of the New Forest. The roads from Christchurch to Lymington and to Salisbury had always been toll-free, and the turnpike era in the New Forest had come to an end by 1850. Nevertheless, many of the gates still existed — at Beaulieu, Brinton, Buckland, Bull Hill, East Boldre, Exbury, Hatchett, Keyhaven, Mark Way and Pilley — and local children demanded pennies from passengers to open them. *Calton Phoenix collection*

'Now about these 'ere tollgates'. Brake No 23 again, in later times — 21 August 1913 — and now in the care of Elliott Bros. Years before, it had probably been converted from an earlier charabanc, whose open sides put outer passengers at considerable risk. Instead, a brake had steps and a safety rail at the rear, a central gangway to the forward-facing seats and enclosed sides. Just three seats were lost in the process. *Peter Delaney collection*

Two- and four-horse brakes of Thomas Elliott's Royal Blue fleet on a pub-crawl to Hall & Woodhouse Blandford Brewery premises in Dorset. These brakes were the first of his vehicles to feature a two-tone livery. They carried a small circular garter enclosing just a capital 'E' on the lower panelling. Elliott's kindly nature was extended to his horses also; they wear earmuffs to protect them from the sun. *Wilts & Dorset*

Thomas Elliott acquired his first coach licence (No 21) for a four-in-hand enclosed vehicle of the revived stage pattern in April 1894. It represented a renewed interest in the use of the type, rather than a continuous link with the mail coaches of pre-railway days. There were places for 24 passengers aboard the vehicle, only six of whom could be squeezed inside. *M. J. Tozer collection*

It is not known when Elliott acquired his first four-in-hand vehicle — a 19-seat charabanc — because the commissioners did not take it upon themselves to license what they termed 'omnibuses' until August 1888. Nevertheless, Elliott had just the one charabanc — a completely roofless carriage — to offer up for an omnibus licence (No 23) at the start, compared with five omnibus licences granted to Laidlaw and three to Ames. Had this charabanc gone to Holmsley before that date? Probably, because the Royal Bath Hotel sent hired 'conveyances' to pick up visitors wherever they wished, provided they first sent a letter or telegram to its secretary, Merton Coates, and Elliott could well have been chosen to do so. However, with this vehicle, which was not a 'coach' in the accepted parlance of the time, he is unlikely to have made the journey until his 'Branksome Mews' came into operation in October 1887. Furthermore, from 6 March 1888, that would no longer have been worthwhile, following the opening of the direct rail link to Christchurch (and Bournemouth) from Brockenhurst via Sway. At the same time, rail tracks between Bournemouth East and West stations came into use, and carriage proprietors needed to look to their hackney cabs for short-haul work within the town.

Throughout the next decade their hackney carriages were

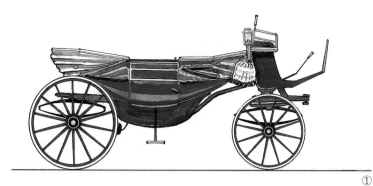

①

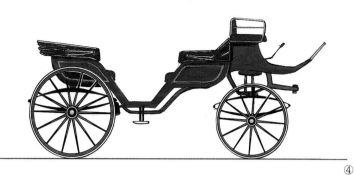

④

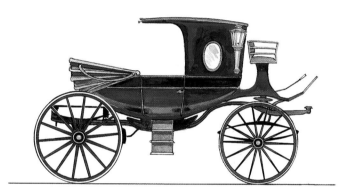

②

⑤

③

Types of hackney carriage (drawn by one horse) licensed to Thomas Elliott at Bournemouth, 1885-1910:

Class 'A' (four passengers plus one beside driver):

1. Landau: largely for summer use only
2. Barouche: spring, autumn and wet weather
3. Brougham: classic 'growler cab' for all-round use
4. Victoria: for showing off high fashion in summer

Class 'C' (two passengers plus driver):

5. Double Chair: developed from the single-seat Bath Chair, which helped give Bournemouth its early image. Operated from the Pier Approach, the double chair was probably unique to the town.

Colin Morris

largely of the type which, in London, would have been called 'growlers'. Rather than the two-wheeled hansom cabs common in the capital, these were four-plus-one-seat four-wheelers, with metal tyres which produced the characteristic 'growl'. The additional seat, open to the elements, was beside the driver. All were drawn by just one horse apiece, the licence fee, at one guinea (£1.05), being but one half of the cost of a two-or-more horse-drawn carriage.

During his entire time in the profession, Thomas Elliott had more hackney carriages than the larger 'omnibuses' in his licensed fleet but, at its zenith during 1899-1901, only just. During that time there were 14, against 11 of the latter. The hackneys comprised nine landaus, together with barouches, victorias and a brougham. There was also a five-seat wagonette capable of conversion to a very small omnibus.

An unknown factor is 'how many other carriages did Elliott possess?' If a vehicle was not plying for hire, but was produced in response to 'private request', there was no requirement for a local authority licence. Among those never in the licensed capacity were dog carts (transverse seats, back-to-back, with a dog-carrying box between, and used for shooting parties), governess carts (very small wagonettes, each usually drawn by a hand-led pony), rally carts (light two-seaters designed to show off driving skills) and phaetons (sporting carriages with two seats and drawn by high-stepping horses).

What today would be called a 'self-drive' facility was also on offer. Additionally, those with sufficient riding ability (and suitably attired for the part) could hire a mount from a stable of well-fed, groomed and trusted horses reserved for that purpose. At a time when there was a Victorian craze for ferneries, one of the features of Bournemouth was its hedges of peat, moss and fern, held together with wickerwork. These were set-off by rhododendron, laurestina (both poisonous to horses), arbutus, myrtle and bay; a trot at a gentle pace along the local carriageways was a popular recreation and a good source of income for Elliott. Riders passing 'through town' could have their horses 'taken in to bait' (provided with water and food) at Branksome Mews, whilst visitors' own private carriages were 'taken into livery' — overnight storage for the vehicle and provender (dried food) and lodging for the horses.

The railways now began to swamp Bournemouth with visitors, with in excess of 10 carriages per train bringing in far more than road coaches ever did. The resident population grew apace to serve the tourists; by 1890 it had passed the 37,000 mark and was still multiplying rapidly — bad news for the famous plants and Decimus Burton's original town plan, but good for the local job-masters. Elliott opened 'Avenue Mews', better known as 'Royal Blue Mews', on the north side of Avenue Lane in 1893, and followed that with 'The Avenue Mews' on the south by 1900, so that he had three mews in close proximity.

Absent for over 30 years, there was now a national resurgence of interest in 'the old coaching days'. Laidlaw alone seems to have retained at least one old stage coach from his early fleet, while others had replicas built. Thomas Elliott was granted Bournemouth licence No 21 for his first in April 1894; this was a 24-seater drawn by four horses, and joined his 'omnibus' fleet of four charabancs, two brakes and two wagonettes. By March 1900 he had three more of similar capacity; Henry Laidlaw (Excelsior) had four, John Trowbridge (Bournemouth Rover) two, George Ames (Tantivy) two, and G. R. Melton (Lansdowne Stables) one, making a total of 13 of this pattern at work in the borough. They were employed in the main on early-start, day-long excursions to Corfe Castle, the New Forest and Wimborne, whereas the charabancs and pair-horse brakes made shorter excursions.

Safety considerations were brought into question, since there were places for only four passengers inside coaches of the stage (or 'park drag') pattern. All the rest travelled on the roof and fore-and-aft boxes, five abreast with the outboard seats on the replicas protruding beyond the width of the bodywork. How such unstable loads were granted licences now seems a mystery. Accidents did happen, and led to a restriction upon seats to those not extending beyond a point directly above the axle hubs. Eventually Elliott took matters into his own hands and cut down two of his coaches so that all their passengers were carried just below driver's seat level. These (Nos 42 and 86) were reclassified as 'coach-charabancs'.

What Bournemouth's Horse Committee referred to as 'omnibuses' were licensed in three categories. For those picking up all their passengers at the same time and fare for a tour or excursion, a Class A licence was issued; travel to and from a railway station required a Class C licence, whilst stage-carriage operation within the borough (a status Bournemouth achieved on 30 June 1890) necessitated a Class B. Elliott held licences for Classes A and B.

The first 'proper' omnibus company, with double-deckers, started on 30 April 1899 with the founding of Bournemouth, Boscombe & Westbourne Omnibus Co Ltd, but a handful of

◄◄ There was a maximum of four stage-coach-pattern vehicles in the Royal Blue fleet by 1900. It is difficult to deduce the identity of each from photographs, since even the wheels (18/16 spokes, 16/14, or 14/12) and liveries were changed from time to time. In use, their fore-and-aft rear-wheel brakes screeched down Poole Hill, and that — together with excessive horn-blowing, and singing passengers — annoyed local residents.
M. J. Tozer collection

In order to please the council, Elliott converted two of his coaches into 'coach-charabancs', by lopping the saloon section and carrying all the passengers at front-seat level. The extra-large acetylene headlamp, carrying a carbide charge of some six hours, shows that this one was on a long out-of-season journey around the New Forest. Coaches were to proceed at a walking pace past Boscombe Tabernacle during divine service, said a local byelaw.
M. J. Tozer collection.

▲ other operators — including Thomas Elliott — dabbled with Class B work, using vehicles not entirely suited for the purpose. In September 1891, Elliott received permission to use one of his two-horse brakes (No 97) on stage-carriage work in town. He followed that by putting top-covers on two small wagonettes and, as late as October 1902, was empowered to use two garden-seated brakes on temporary B licences until the Corporation's electric tramcars started running. He served Boscombe, Winton and Westbourne — and Elizabeth Elliott is said to have acted as a conductress.

Mrs Elliott's major contribution had yet to come. On 20 December 1900, Thomas Elliott joined forces with, among others, two local newspaper proprietors (an astute way to ensure good press coverage) and became Chairman of Tom Elliott Ltd — thus going into a business area twice entered by Laidlaw, between 1877 and 1888, with conspicuous lack of success. A similar fate awaited Elliott. Despite its nominal capital of £4,000 (against Laidlaw's £13,690 called-up 23 years earlier), Tom

Elliott Ltd was wound up on 17 August 1903. Elizabeth, fierce in support of her husband, rode to the rescue. Together with their elder son John T. G. Elliott, she traded as E. Elliott & Son — 'the wife of Thomas Elliott but carrying on business separately from him' — from the Royal Blue Mews, Avenue Lane and Bourne Hall Mews, Queen's Road (near the West station). Mother and son were joined later in this holding operation by the second son, William Edward, until, from 1908, Thomas was once again able to trade under his own name.

It was during this period that John T. G. Elliott (from 1905) and William Edward (from 1906) began to drive the coaches, joining forces with Shadrach Pounds, a particularly stalwart employee who had started with the firm in 1894. Pounds preferred to be known as 'Charlie' — and this name was destined to be displayed on vehicles trading in Bournemouth nearly a full century later. Henry Hayward Elliott, the third son, joined them as a driver in 1909 — and at 18 years, he must have fibbed about his age.

All was never quite the same, however; the fleet was considerably reduced, no loss hurting more than the brake which had proudly borne Licence No 1. In 1910, Thomas took to his bed in a 'long and painful illness' and John (Jack) and William Edward (Ted) began to trade as 'Elliott Bros'. On Saturday 28 January 1911 Thomas Elliott died, aged just 53, at his residence, 'Girvan', in Talbot Road, Winton. Elizabeth mourned her 'own darling Tom' and set about supporting her sons as they carried forward the good name of 'Royal Blue', as a lasting testament to a dearly beloved husband. She would live to see just how successful they would become in that task during the next two decades.

What was the achievement of Thomas Elliott? He was not 'the pioneer of coaching and charabanc excursions', as the local press claimed at his death; they started in Bournemouth a quarter of a century earlier. Nor was his the largest local firm. Both Laidlaw's and Ames' were bigger. Instead, his triumph came through the reputation he gained from the attention he paid to detail, organisation and presentation — and for becoming the foremost four-in-hand whip in the district. He was generous and philanthropic, popular with his staff and, above all, visitors to

Bournemouth, who simply preferred to travel Royal Blue. Finally, whereas Laidlaw's family simply sold up at his death, Thomas and Elizabeth had instilled in their sons a sufficient love of the profession to ensure the great advances which were to follow.

It is worth pausing, for one moment, to consider what effort and expense went into putting 24 fare-paying passengers aboard one of Elliott's top-heavy horse-drawn coaches. Compare that, if you will, with placing a similar number upon the next generation's motor charabancs. A motor vehicle has a fairly limited number of parts, does not 'contaminate' its lodging (beyond a little oil) and can be taken to pieces by a couple of fitters to see what has gone wrong with it.

By contrast, each coach required eight horses allotted to it; four from its home mews and four based as change-teams in several outstations along the day-tour routes. Team horses were not suitable for hauling growlers, nor for private hacking. Moreover, Elliott did his best to ensure that his teams were properly matched: bay, black, brown, chestnut, grey or roan accordingly, with proper conformation for the job —

particularly powerful hindquarters with gait to suit. That meant a lot of horses for different types of use, and at one stage Elliott is said to have had over 200. Their forage (or 'fuel') was a good supply of clean water, a salt lick, oats and beans by the bushel, bran by the sack, and meadow and clover hay by the hundredweight; together with 70lb of bedding straw, the weekly bill for each horse was £1 2s 0d (£1.10). In season, this was supplemented by mangolds, swedes and other green food, plus rented grazing for recuperating horses.

The approximate purchase price for each animal was £70, its value diminishing to £20 after 10 years' service. They suffered illnesses, several of which could be fatal: influenza, heat stroke, strained back sinews, lameness, plant poisoning, parasitic mange, ring bone, fever in the feet, sweet itch, lice, cracked heel, shivering fits, ringworm, eczema, fret, colic, broken wind, gripes, garget, and lampas; moreover, being creatures which liked to establish who was boss, they bit and kicked one another. If one of them caught glanders or farcy, the whole stable had to

be dispersed, limewashed and disinfected. Veterinary surgeon J. T. King was a regular visitor.

The skills required at the various mews were those of saddler, harness repairer, shoesmith, feeder, sweeper and mucker-out, groom, corn and bean-crusher operator, nightwatchman and (since Elliott was also a carriage-builder and repairer) blacksmith, wood-working coachbuilder, coach-plater, wheelwright, cart-greaser, upholsterer and hood-fitter, and lamp-trimmer.

To ease the employment problem, three of Elliott's daughters helped their mother with book-keeping, ordering and selling stock, arranging itineraries and timetables, designing publicity, dealing with correspondence and making up paypackets.

The first, tiller-steered 'motor omnibus' appeared at Bournemouth in September 1899, and a 6hp, single-cylinder hire car before that. This was the start of a new era, but Thomas Elliott did not participate in the transition tackled by a few of his contemporaries; that was a challenge he left to be picked up by his sons.

▲ Twenty-one passengers are seated on the roof and boxes of this coach on a trip to Corfe Castle — and, apparently, none inside. That does not include the driver and the official horn-blower. Complaints about stability and safety led to legislation by the Horse Committee at Bournemouth to restrict the total seating capacity of this type of vehicle to 22. Yet this photograph was taken well after this ruling was made in 1901. *Ian Allan Library*

2. Motor Taxicabs and Charabancs

Perhaps because of the large infrastructure involved in running an exclusively horse-drawn fleet, together with a lingering sentiment for a much-loved father, Jack and Ted Elliott delayed motorising their business. In a marked overlap of technology, they had only horse-drawn carriages to send on their father's behalf to the airshow at the Bournemouth Aviation Ground Aerodrome near Tuckton Cross in June and July 1910 — an event marred by the death of the Hon C. S. Rolls, partner in the Rolls-Royce company, killed when the tail assembly of his aircraft collapsed. Indeed, the brothers had been obliged to watch as Bournemouth rivals Mark Briant, Walter Dinnivan, Henry Beamish and William Wells Graham (the founder of Hants & Dorset Motor Services Ltd) were granted licences to drive motor taxicabs as early as January 1908 — each had to pass a test for the Motor Union Certificate the following year, after complaints about 'the incompetence and inefficiency of many drivers'.

Thus the Elliotts had been in no shape to contest the brief incursion into the town of the Provincial Motor Cab Company's Charron and Wolseley taxis, which arrived in 1909. Fortunately, two yet more serious challenges to their coaching arm failed to materialise: in October 1910 and February 1911, the South Coast Saloon Autobus Company set its sights upon running a saloon motorbus between Bournemouth and Margate, while, later in 1911, Motor Coaches Ltd sought a five-year monopoly for 'a first class service of motor omnibuses, coaches, charabancs, taxicabs and delivery vans for the benefit and convenience' of Bournemouth — which would have put all the local operators out of business had it been granted.

Within a month of the death of their father, the Elliott brothers' stables suffered an outbreak of the dreaded glanders, and they received a meagre £12 from borough funds in respect of a horse destroyed by the veterinary surgeon. They began to sell off the horses and carriages and, in October 1912, purchased a pair of Unic 12/16hp landaulettes, the first of 26 taxicabs of that make delivered to and acquired by them with Bournemouth registrations right through to February 1919. They also tried a 15hp Napier in 1913 and two powerful Studebaker cabriolets in 1915, but returned to the French-built Unic, which proved long-lived and reliable. Thereafter, Wolseleys and Vauxhalls were purchased.

To house their fleet of taxis the brothers acquired the lease of the Lansdowne Stables of G. R. Melton at 229 Old Christchurch Road — the earliest ones having been garaged in the garden of their parents' house in Talbot Road, Winton. From December 1913, unless privately booked from the garage (in which case the previous fare charts applied), all their cabs were obliged to have illuminated taxi-meters fitted which sounded a loud bell to tell the passengers that the clock had started, the charge now being based upon the time it took to get to the destination.

The first motor charabanc service at Bournemouth had been run in February 1906 by Charles Pooss and Percy Parsons with a Durkopp 40hp 2-tonner, which went to Wimborne and other

Jack and Ted Elliott were still running a full programme of horse-drawn excursions when, on 20 March 1913, they at last entered the motor charabanc business with two 28hp Dennis charabancs, both 20-seaters, in a dark blue/sky blue livery. Seen at the foot of Commercial Road, Bournemouth, on 30 July 1913 is the first of the pair, EL 1570 — the very first Royal Blue motor coach.
Alan Lambert collection

The Elliotts began their long association with the products of Daimler on 31 July 1913 with the delivery — in grey — of EL 1833, a 26-seat, 40hp Tylor-engined charabanc. With careful driving, it could achieve 7.6mpg — not too bad for a vehicle which weighed well over 4 tons unloaded. The bodywork was ahead of its time, the doors for each row being on the nearside only.
Alan Lambert collection

15

Tom Elliott's horse-drawn brakes are about to depart from the south side of The Square in the autumn of 1906. On the north side, the motoring era is already well established. A green MMC tiller-steered wagonette of the Canford Cliffs Motor Omnibus Co is parked in front of EL 429 and EL 384, two Durkopps of 'The Tourist' run by Charles Pooss, pioneer of Bournemouth's motor charabancs.
Colin Morris collection

Elliott Bros' taxi fleet grew to be one of the largest in the town. By 1924 it had been augmented by luxurious hire-cars, driven by uniformed chauffeurs. There were 30 such cars, of which 20 were 'Silent Knight' 30hp Daimlers, and six Rolls-Royces. Illustrated upon an Elliott Bros brochure is a Rolls-Royce 40/50hp cabriolet, the stable-mate of some landaulettes by the same illustrious manufacturer.
Colin Billington collection

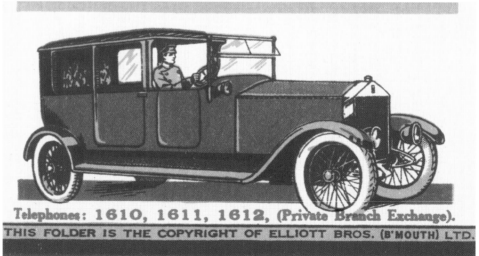

Telephones: 1610, 1611, 1612, (Private Branch Exchange).
THIS FOLDER IS THE COPYRIGHT OF ELLIOTT BROS. (B'MOUTH) LTD.

local attractions under the fleetname 'The Tourist' from a stand at the northwest corner of The Square. The 'we were first' syndrome commenced when Mark Briant's executors, who started with a 30hp Lacre some six years later, claimed that theirs was the first 'proper' charabanc service — whatever that meant. But the importance to the Royal Blue story of the latter is that they sold three Daimlers to the firm at the end of the 1921 season. Even the Elliotts' old family friend, Albert Futcher, who traded as 'Empress', had a Commer 34hp charabanc on the road by November 1912, before the brothers at last bought the first of what they always called 'motor coaches'.

The first motor coaches to be based at a hastily-adapted Royal Blue Mews, Avenue Lane, were two wooden-wheeled Dennis 3-ton charabancs bought in March 1913. In keeping with the horse-drawn vehicles beside which they served, they were finished in the traditional dark blue livery — the only ones in the Royal Blue motor charabanc fleet to be so painted. Apart from the original one, which was temporarily grey, all five Daimler 4-tonners purchased before the outbreak of World War 1 arrived

in a sky-blue livery from the Bournemouth works of Ransom & Whitehead. EL 2001, delivered in June 1914, was the first fitted with the remarkable Silent Knight sleeve-valve engine, which would be a Daimler feature for the best part of 20 years. The sky-blue livery was set to continue (albeit later with dark blue trim) until 1927.

Like operators nationwide, Elliott Bros had acquired the seven prewar vehicles under a Government subsidy scheme in which the purchaser gambled that the deteriorating political situation in Europe would get no worse. Regrettably, it did, and the Army Service Corps and the Lords Commissioners of the Admiralty (for the Royal Navy Air Service) called up all but one of the vehicles plus their drivers. The two Dennis charabancs saw just two summers in the service of Elliott Bros, and one of the Daimlers was in their possession for less than two weeks — whilst EL 1833 remained a civilian.

The Elliotts were obliged to emulate fledgling omnibus companies throughout Britain during the conflict and buy a make of chassis not upon the military's 'wanted' list. They

Daimler EL 2000 and Dennis EL 1570, now painted sky blue overall, flank brand-new EL 2001, the first of Elliott's famous 'Silent Knight' Daimlers, in June 1914. The 'Silent Knight' was a sleeve-valve (rather than poppet-valve) engine; it used rather a lot of oil and the valves required regular replacement, but saved fuel and created a good impression with its quiet running. Vehicles so fitted became very popular.
Philip Davies collection

managed to obtain a total of 15 American-built Selden chassis over a 14-month period from May 1915, with their own workforce bodying several of them in rented accommodation once occupied by Henry Laidlaw at the Royal Mews, Norwich Road. The Seldens were something of a mixed blessing, not least because the manufacturer was still fitting wooden wheels, which created a dreadful racket during the summer months as the spokes shrank and worked loose in their sockets. Nightly removal and soaking in water proved necessary. Nevertheless, two (EL 2627/8) were fitted with enclosed Pullman bodywork in December for continued winter use. Others were temporarily rebodied as lorries as the tourist trade began to suffer.

The Defence of the Realm Act which saw the loss of the Dennis and Daimler vehicles was followed by a series of Emergency Provisions, notably the restriction of vehicle movements not directly connected with the war effort, and the strict rationing of petrol. In July 1915, the acquisition of three licences and two De Dions transferred from Walter Dinnivan's Westbourne Garage (conveniently already painted in pale blue), saw the Royal Blue complement of charabancs rise to eight, becoming for the first time the largest in Bournemouth. The

restrictions in force dampened the family's celebrations somewhat, but this was the point at which they began to outstrip their rivals. By the following summer they also possessed the town's largest motor taxicab fleet, but again all was far from plain sailing; all 12 applications for their licences were turned down that June — and only four for Royal Blue charabancs were granted. The brothers tried paraffin as fuel, a device stubbornly rejected by the Seldens.

Despite being a member of the Hampshire Carabiniers Volunteers before the war, Jack Elliott — beset by a chest problem — was directed instead into military aeroplane components work, sub-contracted to the Grahame-White Aviation Co Ltd. The other two brothers were called up, Harry Elliott serving at the Central Flying School of the Royal Flying Corps/Royal Air Force, and Ted with the Royal Naval Air Service. Tragically, the latter went missing in his seaplane in 1917. Thereafter, 'Elliott Bros' meant John T. G. and Henry Hayward Elliott.

Before wartime restrictions began to bite, the changeover to motor charabancs had enabled the Elliotts to extend their touring range considerably: Weymouth, Sherborne, Shaftesbury,

In World War 1, all bar one of Elliott Bros' motor charabancs were requisitioned for military service, and deliveries of British-made chassis simply dried up. As a stop-gap, 15 wooden-wheeled American-built Selden chassis were acquired and bodied locally. The Selden was powered by a 35hp engine and, fully fitted, weighed no more than 2¾ tons — but this advantage did not seem to enhance its performance.
Alan Lambert collection

Early wartime difficulties were eased in July 1915 with the acquisition of the licences and two De Dion charabancs of Walter Dinnivan, a Westbourne tours and excursions proprietor. Still in Dinnivan's service on 6 August 1913, EL 1718, a 25hp De Dion, was about to depart from Avenue Road with a party for Wimborne at 3s (15p) per head. The time-keeping town sergeant is in attendance.
Precious Memories

Between April 1919 and at least June 1923, Elliott Bros employed fleetnumbers with added letter suffixes. Other than a device to keep the numbers below a dozen per batch, there is still speculation as to what this scheme was designed to do. A and B were Daimler 30hp Y-type of 1919; C Daimler 22hp CK-type and, probably, one Y-type of 1920; D Daimler 30hp Y-type of 1921; E Daimler 30hp Y-type of 1922; and F a mixture of Crossley 14-seaters and Daimler Y-type of 1923. To complicate matters, the registration cards for Bournemouth's EL 5805-9999 and RU 1-4032 went missing years ago, but pictures of Royal Blue vehicles not on the recorded fleet list within that range are still coming to light.

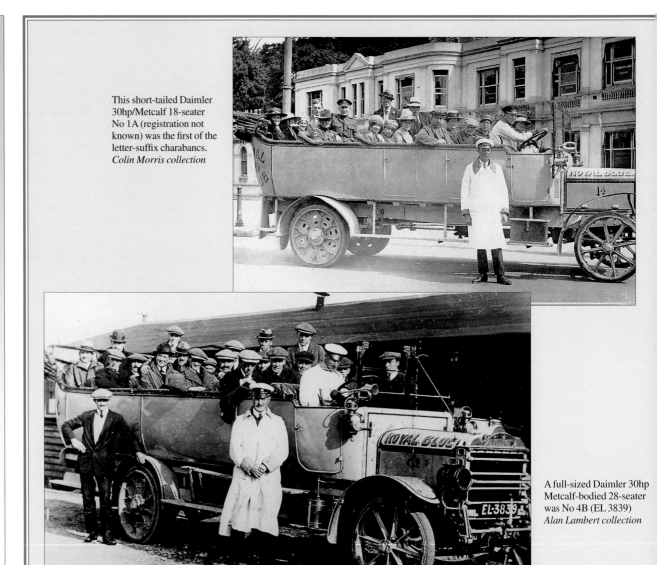

This short-tailed Daimler 30hp/Metcalf 18-seater No 1A (registration not known) was the first of the letter-suffix charabancs. *Colin Morris collection*

A full-sized Daimler 30hp Metcalf-bodied 28-seater was No 4B (EL 3839) *Alan Lambert collection*

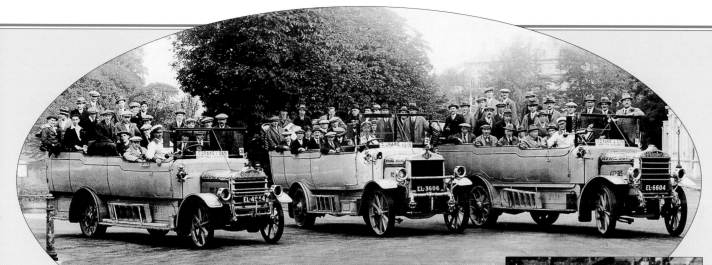

AEC YC No 9
(EL 3606) of 1919 is
flanked by Daimler CK
No 2C (EL 4944) of 1920
and Daimler Y No 2E
(EL 6604) of 1922.
Peter Delaney collection

A fine close-up of Ransom &Whitehead-
bodied Daimler Y-type No 2D (thought to be
EL 5979). *Colin Morris collection*

Crossley 14-seater No 1F (EL 760 ?) of 1923,
with two Unic taxicabs, probably also belonging
to Elliott Bros. *Colin Morris collection*

Stonehenge, Salisbury and Southampton had been added to the day-trip itinerary, and accommodation in Wharf Road (now Wharfdale Road), on the north side of the West station, had been rented in anticipation of an increased fleet. That expansion had to wait, however; the last public service vehicle delivered in Bournemouth during World War 1 was Elliott Bros' Selden EL 3121 in July 1916. Jack and Harry Elliott became members of the Motor Engineering Section of Bournemouth Chamber of Trade in 1918 and planned to take the lead locally when new machines were once again available and Petrol Regulations allowed. The Horse Committee (still so named) decided that 50 Class A licences (for tours and excursions) would be issued — and 19 of these would go to Elliott Bros. The next largest number was six for Bournemouth & District Motor Services Ltd (Hants & Dorset) — and it only had two charabancs on the road at the time.

Vehicle supplies were resumed in March 1919, Elliott Bros' EL 3603, one of six AEC YC chassis, being the first; some were bodied by Ransom & Whitehead while others were said to have been constructed locally to a Grahame-White design at a now-redundant military aircraft works — an arrangement which apparently led to the Elliotts' taking over the Rutland Road premises in Winton.

The completed vehicles were stored ready for the first postwar season at the Royal Mews, where Bournemouth & District had become the new nominal landlord. The latter had acquired the leasehold previously held by G. R. Melton Ltd, thus making Royal Blue its tenant in that property. Sensing that Bournemouth & District was becoming a force to be reckoned with, Jack Elliott suggested that Royal Blue should share in the business. However, he meant just the bus business, and was not prepared to include his firm's charabancs, so discussion was short. Nevertheless, he had given the first hint that the Elliotts were contemplating stage-carriage work also. It was the first of several exchanges of the kind initiated by Jack Elliott.

An order for 15 of Elliott Bros' preferred Daimler 'Silent Knight' chassis had been placed and these were delivered in June to participate in a bumper season, when demand was greatly in excess of supply, and up to 100 potential excursionists were frequently left standing disappointed in The Square. The fleet was increased by a further two Daimlers when the Bournemouth Motor Syndicate, of 109 Christchurch Road, ceased operating before it really got started. Its third Daimler went to Charlie Pounds, who had set up on his own account that spring, initially in West Hill Place, as 'Charlie's Cars'. He was destined to go from strength to strength without ever treading upon Elliott toes.

The Horse Committee's response to the underestimated demand was to grant the Elliotts 27 touring licences in 1919. Yet it was a political upheaval that September which set Royal Blue upon an unforeseen path — the provision of express coach services. The National Union of Railwaymen called a national strike in response to the Lloyd George Government's proposals to reduce wages across the board. It was short and sharp: the Government quickly acceded to the railwaymen's terms, but the Elliotts were among several charabanc operators within range of London to satisfy the needs of stranded travellers with runs to the capital. It soon became clear that here was a demand sufficient to establish such journeys on a regular basis the following year.

Initially the service ran from Bournemouth on Fridays and Saturdays and returned from the Thomas Cook office in Pall Mall, London, every Saturday and Monday, at £1 single and £1 10s 0d (£1.50) return, reduced thereafter to 17s 6d (87½p) single and, by August 1922, 15s (75p) and £1 5s 0d (£1.25) return — considerably less than the train fare. The Elliotts acquired an office and garage at 68/70 Holdenhurst Road to cope with this additional arm of their enterprise.

Postwar Daimler deliveries recommenced in April 1919 with No 11 (EL 3731), a 30hp model. It is posed together with a later Ransom & Whitehead-bodied example (EL 3837) on the Mendip Hills during a trip to Cheddar Caves — a popular Royal Blue destination — with a Dalton's of Bournemouth private-hire outing. In 1919, the town council decreed that iron stays should reinforce offside coachwork.
Andrew Waller collection

Elliott Bros re-wheeled its fleet in 1923, fitting what were at first known as 'balloon tyres'. These not only reduced wear and tear generally and gave the passengers a smoother ride, but greatly enhanced the appearance of existing vehicles — as Daimler/Metcalf No 5A (EL 3737) demonstrates on a shopfitters' staff outing. It was some while, however, before punctures became infrequent.
Alan Lambert collection

23

Similarly, public demand quickly led to a remarkable expansion in the tours sector. In 1920, a long-distance, seven-day tours programme was started in conjunction with Thomas Cook & Sons as agents. Stage-by-stage visits to Devon & Cornwall, the Wye Valley & Shakespeare Country and the Lake District were followed by what was seen as an audacious trip to Edinburgh — all still upon solid tyres. Initially to meet a request from members of the Bolton Co-operative Society, whose members each paid two guineas (£2.10) for their tickets, a trip around the Isle of Wight was arranged — the charabancs going across to the island on barges from Lymington to Yarmouth — and this became established as a seasonal 'Around the Island Tour'. It was so well patronised that in 1921 the fare was lowered to 30s (£1.50) from Bournemouth and, the following year, to 21s (£1.05). In time for the 1922 season, materials left spare from the extension of the Rutland Road garage were used to erect a six-vehicle dormy-shed at Yarmouth, thus removing the costly business of shipping charabancs across the Solent. The tour went clockwise around the island, with a stop at the Station Hotel, Ryde, for lunch. Also in 1922, patrons were invited to take their picnic hampers on a 40-mile Bournemouth-New Forest excursion leaving at 10.30am and returning at 6pm, all for 3s 6d (17½p) — very little more than one old penny (0.41p) per passenger mile.

Elliott Bros now operated 55 of the 85 coaches licensed to some 13 firms in the town, but Charlie Pounds stole a small march by introducing a 14-seat coach to his fleet fitted with pneumatic tyres. Robert Symes followed suit and went one better by fitting them to a Dennis 40hp charabanc of his 'Enterprise' fleet — the first 4-ton public service vehicle in Bournemouth so equipped, or so he said! A. E. Ransom told the journal *Modern Transport* that his 'Bournemouth Rambler' Leyland was the first (and with white-walled tyres too!). For that he had 'suffered quite a lot of criticism and some derision'. Ah well!

Never upstaged for long, the Elliotts forthwith commenced an expensive re-wheeling of their fleet and had most of them converted in time for the 1923 season, by which time their London coaches were being followed by a Crossley tender, also on pneumatics, which carried their passengers' luggage. Additionally, six Crossley 14-seat charabancs were purchased, and some Daimlers still on solids continued the winter haulage work. Others began providing a mildly provocative fortnightly service 'from all parts' to the home games of Bournemouth & Boscombe Athletic FC.

In late November 1923, the Elliott family visited the Commercial Motor Show at Olympia and saw exhibited a 'quadruple purpose' coach body newly designed by London Lorries Ltd of Kentish Town. It was capable of being used in four different modes: a) fully enclosed; b) with hood folded back, but with windows left standing as side-screens; c) hood erected with windows down; or d) hood folded and windows down as a completely open vehicle. They were immediately impressed and an order was placed with London Lorries Ltd to rebody existing Daimlers and equip new ones entering the fleet — all of which were on pneumatics. The vehicles were 24-seaters and started entering service in 1924, forming the mainstay of the fleet for some four years.

Elliott Bros was among those which carried out experiments with wireless (radio) for use on coaches. No 5C was adapted and fitted by Brights Ltd of Bournemouth with a Gecophone two-valve set with three stages and low-frequency amplification. It had a range of up to 100 miles and, on Friday 25 May 1923, during a run to Wimborne Minster, the passengers have donned earphones to listen to a broadcast concert from Cardiff, heard quite clearly.

No 12D (thought to be EL 6083), on a trip from Bournemouth to Southsea, makes a stop at Swanwick for the passengers to buy chip-baskets of strawberries, fresh from the local fields. This charabanc was one of the first to be re-fitted with disc wheels and pneumatic tyres, in time for the 1923 season. Bringing up the rear, and still on solids, is a Dennis saloon of Tutt's from Gosport, destined to be acquired by Hants & Dorset the following summer.
Alan Lambert collection

This unusual shot of EL 3734, rebodied by London Lorries and minus its Beatonson hood, but with side screens in place, demonstrates the transition from charabanc proper to coach. Six separate doors for access to the seats have been replaced by gaps between them and only two doors, both on the nearside. Additionally, electric headlights and sidelights are now standard and, by 1925, the livery had become two-tone.
Alan Lambert collection

Royal Blue had become a limited-liability company (for the second time) on 18 May 1921 with a nominal capital of £20,000. Its registered office was at 68 Holdenhurst Road, and John, Henry and Elizabeth Elliott were the directors of the reconstituted firm, Elliott Bros (Bournemouth) Ltd. Harry Rollings was appointed General Manager, A. E. Krinks Secretary, and C. Fletcher Chief Engineer, based at Rutland Road. In a bet-hedging exercise before the express service flourished, Elliott Bros now sought to run stage-carriage services in and around Bournemouth. Jack Elliott, Rollings and a local motor dealer went to France to visit a British military store of vehicles, and purchased 14 AEC and Daimler chassis which were then refurbished into 12 sound 'Daimler' units. These in turn were sent to Dodson's of Willesden where that firm's patent 'charabus' bodies were fitted, and painted pale blue.

The first thing that Hants & Dorset knew about this was in August 1921 when Elliott Bros was granted 12 omnibus licences by the Horse Committee to run to Lymington, Ringwood and Wimborne. At this point, Jack Elliott became seriously ill and went to a clinic in Switzerland to recuperate. Harry and his mother decided not to proceed until September 1923 when they asked for 10 licences. Hants & Dorset promptly requested 30 charabanc licences. The Committee declined both, and Elliott Bros agreed to sell all 12 vehicles (three on pneumatics, the rest on solids) to Hants & Dorset for £11,000; the latter had them registered and painted green, and promised not to take any interest in charabancs, cars or taxicabs within 10 miles of Bournemouth Square for a period of 21 years from 1 November 1923. It also asked the Elliotts to remove their charabancs from the remaining part of the Royal Mews, but

briefly considered letting them St Michael's Road garage instead — which didn't happen.

One of Jack Elliott's first actions upon his return was to seek, in February 1924, an amalgamation between Royal Blue and Hants & Dorset (charabancs included this time, presumably), which the latter declined, thus underlining the recently agreed division of traffic interests. The relative decks having been cleared (albeit a shade reluctantly), the Elliotts concentrated their efforts upon the expansion of their already remarkable tours and express operations. In the latter, particularly, they had another stroke of good fortune. The General Strike of May 1926, called in support of the miners, stopped the trains once again and, because Elliott Bros did not employ union labour, led to further groups of rescued passengers sampling the joys of cheap road transport to London, which for many of them became a habit thereafter.

The increased custom saw as many as 40 Royal Blue coaches per day at times on the Bournemouth-London road. Some vehicles were now based in the capital, operating a six-day tour, arranged by Thomas Cook & Son Ltd, to Exeter, Torquay, Dartmoor, Truro, Falmouth, Penzance, Land's End, The Lizard, Clovelly, Barnstaple, Lynton, Minehead, Glastonbury, Cheddar and Wells, and an eight-day tour, leaving London each Saturday, passing through Guildford, Winchester, the New Forest, Lulworth, Swanage, Corfe Castle, Salisbury, Stonehenge, Cheddar and Wells, and making a complete circuit of the Isle of Wight, before returning via Basingstoke.

On 26 February 1927, *Modern Transport* described the Royal Blue fleet as consisting chiefly of Daimlers, of which 34 were Y-type 26-seaters, 20 CK-types with 14- to 16-seat coachwork,

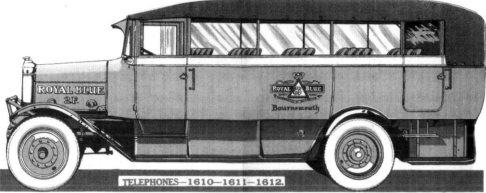

The Royal Blue fleet of coaches in 1924 stood at over 60 vehicles, of which 75% had been fitted with 'quadruple purpose' all-weather bodies by London Lorries Ltd of Kentish Town. As demonstrated by Daimler CK No 2F, a completely open charabanc could have its windows fitted as side screens (above), or, with its Beatonson hood fitted, become a fully-enclosed vehicle. The other mode was with hood, but no windows. *Colin Billington collection*

with other coaches on AEC chassis, some fitted with 'the new 5 type engine'. The fleet of pleasure cars comprised eight Rolls-Royces, 22 six-cylinder Daimlers and eight six-cylinder Wolseleys. A Rolls-Royce chassis was equipped as an emergency service-truck, and was occasionally used to remove damaged engines and fit replacement units at the roadside. Accommodation for 16 coaches was provided in Holdenhurst Road, 20 at the Lansdowne Garage (as the scale of taxi work was being run down) and — according to the amount of work being carried out at the time — space for between 60 and 100 coaches at the Rutland Road premises in Winton. The maintenance and repair shops in the three buildings located here included sections for machine tools, fitters' benches, a smithy, coachbuilders,

painting and trimming, together with a large store of spares which always contained enough parts to build up an entire replacement chassis if such were needed.

It was during this period also that Elliott Bros began to establish a series of leasehold and rented offices and combined sweetshops/newsagents/tobacconists/Royal Blue booking offices in the area, including the then 228 Ashley Road in Parkstone, 2 Richmond Hill, 24 Commercial Road and 93B St Michael's Road in Bournemouth, and 881 Christchurch Road and the Savoy Picture House in Boscombe, all of which, in varying degrees, served to provide yet more custom for a firm whose fame and reputation was about to be spread even farther afield.

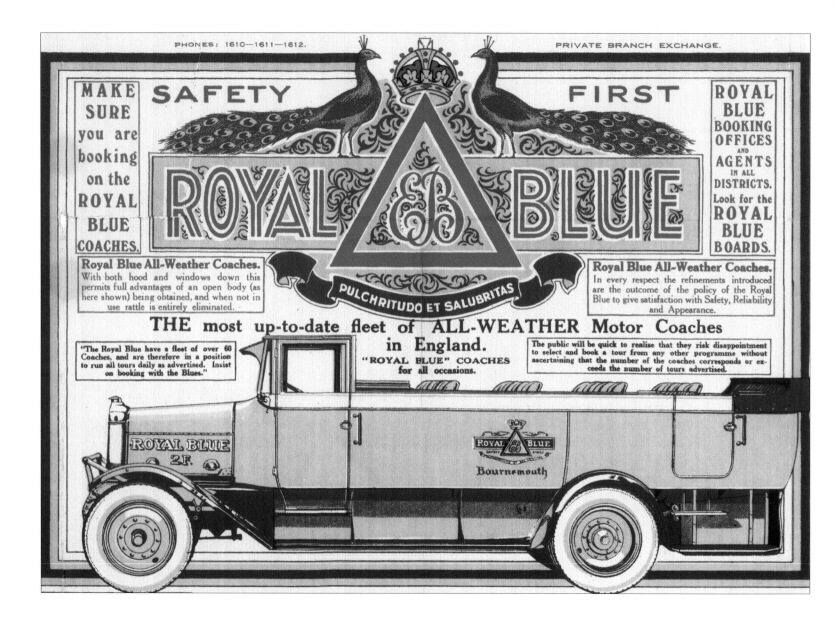

3. Royal Blue Automobile Services

Until 1927, Elliott Bros remained content to develop just its one Bournemouth-London route into a 'proper' express service with intermediate pick-up and set-down points. At the London end, facilities were improved that year by its having become a member of London Coastal Coaches Ltd, founded in April 1925 to apportion mileage, fares and general arrangements in the capital on behalf of its constituent firms. LCC's first Chairman was Bert Smith of National Omnibus & Transport, and later the first General Manager of both Southern and Western National, until they were reorganised by Tilling in 1932. Meanwhile, in the autumn of 1928, Elliott Bros had adopted the trading name 'Royal Blue Automobile Services'. Initially, that title referred to the express work only, but tours and excursions literature shows that it was soon in general use.

Membership of LCC did not insulate Royal Blue from non-associate operators, as Bournemouth became one of the most popular tourist destinations. Causing equal alarm to both Hants & Dorset and Royal Blue was the news, in February 1927, that (the later associated) Greyhound Motors Ltd of Bristol was about to operate a through service to Weymouth and another to Bournemouth, the latter on two routes via Salisbury and Shaftesbury. Hants & Dorset was soon appeased by a clause which precluded Greyhound from plying for hire between those places and Bournemouth, whilst Elliott Bros hastened to raise capital sufficient to establish itself upon express routes to the west and north of its home town — a process accelerated by news that moves were afoot to regularise such traffic nationwide.

In order to achieve this major territorial expansion, Elliott Bros made an early request, in the autumn of 1927, for 26 of the Associated Daimler Company's 424-type low-loading chassis which, despite still being of forward-control configuration, left behind the 20-year-old 'charabanc' image and ushered in a new era of Royal Blue luxury. With the exception of nine built by Hall Lewis, coachwork was by Duple and, thanks to the efficiency of the fastening between the sunshine hood and the window frames, the deep-cushioned seats incorporated moquette upholstery. The detailed specifications for these and all other Royal Blue coaches up to 1930 was drawn up by Jack Elliott and C. Fletcher, the firm's Chief Engineer. The elegant ADC 424s reintroduced the original dark blue livery beloved of

◄◄ Centrepiece of a 1924 Elliott Bros publicity folder: pride of place goes to the ornate fleetname-display worn upon the vehicles in the middle 'twenties. There seems to have been a precedent for NBC's rather inappropriate red 'Royal Blue' fleetname half a century later. *Pulchritudo et Salubritas* (beauty and health) was pinched from the Bournemouth coat of arms to complete an impressive logo. *Colin Billington collection*

◄ When Elliott Bros' service to London became extremely popular, with up to 40 coaches on the road at at time, several second-hand Daimler Y chassis were rebodied and pressed into service. They included LR 8007 (RU 1440) from Hants & Dorset and HO 6175/6 and HO 9696 from Aldershot & District. Then, in 1928, the Elliotts took delivery of 26 ADC 424 sunshine-saloon coaches, five bodied by Hall Lewis and the rest by Duple, including RU 6728. *Colin Morris collection*

Thomas Elliott, and which was to survive upon Royal Blue coaches in service for a further half-century.

Hall Lewis was the coachbuilder chosen to provide the bodywork for six ADC 426 coaches which entered service in July 1928. These were the firm's first forward-control vehicles and the first with fixed head, and roof-racks for passengers' luggage. They also featured double doors and a toilet at the rear — which proved a little too close for nearby passengers' comfort and was soon removed in favour of 'convenience stops' along the way — and were the prototypes for the 25 AEC Reliances with Duple coachwork which followed.

Until April 1928, Elliott Bros' Royal Blue express coaches terminating in London were obliged to wait at roadside stands near the offices of Thomas Cook. A temporary coach station was

then provided in Lupus Street, near Vauxhall Bridge. Pending the opening of Victoria Coach Station in 1932, this uncovered yard, alternately dusty or muddy, served as the awkward base for an otherwise smooth operation. In addition to its long-established Bournemouth route, Elliott Bros commenced services from Lupus Street to Plymouth via Salisbury and to Weston-super-Mare via Bristol, soon after the opening of the yard. In addition, services from Bournemouth to Plymouth via Dorchester and to Ilfracombe via Yeovil started that year. Royal Blue express services from Bournemouth to Birmingham via Coventry and to Bristol via Salisbury followed in 1929.

In October 1928, Elliott Bros had sought licences from councils in Sussex and Kent for a through service from Bournemouth to Margate. Southdown promptly approached

Hants & Dorset with proposals for a joint service between Bournemouth and Brighton. When William Graham of Hants & Dorset went to a meeting with Southdown at Brighton the following month, the eastern terminus under consideration had become — with the approval of the East Kent Road Car Co Ltd — Margate. Probably because of its 1924 agreement with Elliott Bros and so as not to compromise early discussions about the building of a joint Hants & Dorset/Royal Blue terminal at Bournemouth, Hants & Dorset declined the invitation to participate. Elliott Bros launched its Bournemouth-Portsmouth-Brighton-Margate service in April 1929.

Southdown, East Kent and, in the early days, Wilts & Dorset started a joint rival service (between Dover and Bournemouth) on 1 June 1929, but Royal Blue had already established its image strongly enough to enjoy a continuing profit along the South Coast route. Later that month, Elliott Bros signed an agreement with Hants & Dorset for the lease of the lower part of the proposed omnibus station to be built in the centre of Bournemouth. More remarkably, in November of that year, and prompted by the uncertainty surrounding the forthcoming Transport Bill in Parliament, Elliott Bros offered to sell its entire Royal Blue operation to Hants & Dorset. This was declined because Jack and Harry Elliott stipulated that, as part of the deal, they should be given managerial appointments to continue running such work.

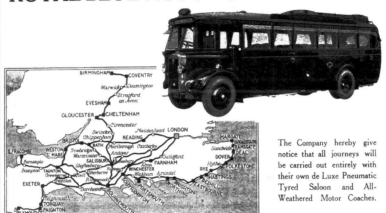

For BOURNEMOUTH and SOUTH-WEST ENGLAND ROYAL BLUE AUTOMOBILE SERVICES

The Company hereby give notice that all journeys will be carried out entirely with their own de Luxe Pneumatic Tyred Saloon and All-Weathered Motor Coaches.

FULL SUMMER PROGRAMME

LONDON, EXETER, TORQUAY & PLYMOUTH .. .. .. via Salisbury, Shaftesbury, Yeovil, etc.
LONDON, EXETER, TORQUAY & PLYMOUTH .. via Winchester, Southampton, Bournemouth, Dorchester, etc.
LONDON, BATH, BRISTOL & WESTON-SUPER-MARE .. via Maidenhead, Reading, Newbury, etc.
LONDON, SOUTHAMPTON & BOURNEMOUTH,
        via Basingstoke, Winchester and the New Forest, etc. (3 times Daily).
LONDON, SOUTHAMPTON & BOURNEMOUTH,
        via Kingston, Guildford, Farnham, Alton, Alresford and Romsey.
LONDON, SALISBURY & SALISBURY PLAIN CAMPS .. .. and all Towns en route (Twice Daily).
BOURNEMOUTH, BATH, BRISTOL & WESTON-SUPER-MARE,
        via Blandford, Shaftesbury, Salisbury, etc. (Twice Daily).
BOURNEMOUTH, TAUNTON, BRIDGWATER, ILFRACOMBE & WESTON-SUPER-MARE,
        via Blandford, Sturminster, Newton, Sherborne, Yeovil, Ilchester, etc. (Twice Daily).
BOURNEMOUTH, BRIDPORT, EXETER, TORQUAY & PLYMOUTH .. .. .. (Twice Daily).
BOURNEMOUTH, GLOUCESTER, CHELTENHAM & BIRMINGHAM,
        via Salisbury, Swindon, Cirencester, Stratford-on-Avon, Leamington Spa, Warwick and Coventry.
BOURNEMOUTH, PORTSMOUTH, BRIGHTON, EASTBOURNE, FOLKESTONE, DOVER
& MARGATE .. .. via Chichester, Worthing, Hastings, Deal and Ramsgate.
THE VERY LATEST TYPE 6-CYL. DAIMLER AND A.E.C. SALOON AND SEMI-SALOON COACHES USED EXCLUSIVELY ON THESE SERVICES, AND FITTED WITH FOUR WHEEL AND SERVO LATEST HYDRAULIC BRAKES.
        See Company's small handbills, obtainable from any Agent, or pages 13, 21, 22, 24, 25 and 30 in this Time-table.

LONDON BOOKING OFFICES AND AGENTS.

Messrs. The London Coastal Coaches, Ltd., 7B, Lower Belgrave Street, Victoria.   'PHONE: Sloane 5291 (and all sub-agencies).
The District Messenger & Theatre Ticket Co.'s Office. (Open Day and Night.) Or any Office. See list under Booking Agents' Aanouncements.   'PHONE: Mayfair 0509.
Nelsons Express Co., Ltd.   'PHONE: Gerrard 8343.
Messrs. Pickfords and all Branches.

Messrs. Keith Prowse & Co., Ltd. and all Branches, 42-43, Poland Street, W.1.   'PHONE: Gerrard 9001.
John Barker & Co., Kensington High St.   'PHONE: 5432 Western.
Messrs. G. B. Tours Ltd., 72, Great Portland Street (and all sub-agencies).   'PHONE: Museum 6831.
Messrs. Thos. Tilling Ltd., 71, High Street, Peckham (and all Branches).   'PHONE: Rodney 4522.

All Drivers and Coaches have undergone Police Authority tests and been approved by them. Each coach is tested periodically by the Police Authorities and is therefore guaranteed safe.   All Hand Luggage is carried free of charge on the Coach.

BOOKING OFFICES AND AGENTS IN ALL TOWNS EN ROUTE.
ILLUSTRATED BROCHURE—12-page folder maps of routes and time-tables can be obtained post free upon request to :
Messrs. ELLIOTT BROTHERS (Bournemouth) LTD.,
68-70, HOLDENHURST ROAD, BOURNEMOUTH. 'PHONE: 1610-1611-1612. OR ANY OFFICE OR AGENT.

The six ADC 426 coaches were converted to full AEC Reliance specification after two seasons' use. They were thus brought into line with 25 Duple-bodied Reliances delivered during 1929. These arrived with two differing roof styles — the earlier ones with a free-standing oval case lettered 'RB' above the indicator. This illustration and the map were featured in a May 1929 announcement of Elliott Bros' services.
Philip Davies collection

The second type of canopy on the Reliances comprised a less wind-resistant design, in which 'Royal Blue' was faired in above the indicator — a preferred style upon subsequent types also. RU 8821 of June 1929 was operating on the twice-daily run to Torquay from Bournemouth; it is emerging from the narrow Charmouth road tunnel under Thistle Hill, once a hazard on what is now the A35. *Ian Allan Library*

Before the Road Traffic Act of 1930 simplified licensing procedures, it was necessary for local police authorities, through whose territory a route passed, to test and approve the coaches and drivers concerned. Each affixed its own metal, stencilled or enamelled badge to the vehicle. Thus, the rear of AEC Reliance RU 8802 bears the visible approval of Arundel, Bath, Brighton, Bristol, Bournemouth, Eastbourne, London Metropolitan, Margate, Portsmouth and Swindon. *Colin Morris collection*

Within a year, Royal Blue had to weather a further flurry of opposition from both external and locally-based express service operators: Ransom & Whitelock's Shamrock & Rambler (and Keith & Boyle of London, who later controlled it), Link Safety Coaches (Bournemouth) Ltd, Olympic Motor Services Ltd of Portsmouth, Modern Travel Ltd of Southampton, Tourist Motor Coaches (Southampton) Ltd, and Highways Ltd, George Ewer & Co Ltd and A. Timpson & Sons Ltd of London were among the firms concerned. The National Omnibus & Transport Co — in the process of transforming itself (in southwest England) into Western National Omnibus Co and Southern National Omnibus Co — also operated express services to several destinations in the West Country but, because of its membership of London Coastal Coaches Ltd, relations with Royal Blue remained cordial to the extent that National provided it with booking facilities.

The division of National was an outcome of the decision of the 'Big Four' railway companies to buy into the existing British Automobile Traction and Tilling-controlled bus companies, rather than run their own competing road services. Railway directors tended to exercise a degree of separateness on bus company boards and this led, in January 1931, to two companies competing for some five months against Royal Blue, at the request of the Southern Railway. From Torquay, the Devon General Omnibus & Touring Co Ltd ran to Bournemouth, where Greyhound Motors Ltd, by then a subsidiary of Bristol Tramways & Carriage Co Ltd, provided connections along Royal Blue's traditional route to London. Royal Blue was in this instance rescued by one of the benefits of the Road Traffic Act 1930, when the recently-appointed Traffic Commissioners refused to renew the Devon General/Greyhound licences for these roads, granting them instead to Royal Blue.

The complete reorganisation of the road licensing system under the provisions of the 1930 Act removed, among other things, the need to approach every local authority along the

Reliance RU 8814 pauses in Botley Square, Hampshire, en route from Bournemouth to Margate, on the South Coast route pioneered by Elliott Bros in April 1929, in the brief period before Southdown and East Kent started a competing service. A notice board beside the Dolphin Hotel, at the left, poses an interesting question. It advertises local tours, which could be booked there, by the Elliotts' Bournemouth-based rival, Shamrock & Rambler.
Colin Morris collection

routes for permission to use the roads under their jurisdiction.
Each had demanded to inspect all vehicles likely to pass its way
and issued an enamel badge to be attached to the rear panelling.
Stage-carriage buses and local taxicabs normally received just
the one, but over the previous three years particularly, long-
distance express coaches had been liberally plastered with them
— and Royal Blue was no exception.

Successor to the AEC Reliance in the Royal Blue fleet was the
Daimler CF6, bodied by Duple and delivered in three batches in
June 1929, and June and July 1930. At the close of the 1929
season, Elliott Bros ordered a comparative batch of four vehicles
each fitted with specially-commissioned Duple 'crash-proof'
bodywork. Following a side-impact from a motorist who
claimed he hadn't noticed a Royal Blue coach in the dark, five
beading strips, initially painted yellow, were incorporated over
reinforced side and rear panelling at wheel level. The four
triallists were an AEC Regal, a Maudslay ML6, a Daimler CF6

and a Leyland Tiger TS2. Fifteen Daimler CF6 (the two 1930
batches) and 18 AEC Regal coaches so-fitted joined the fleet as
a result of these road trials.

The sole Leyland Tiger (LJ 875), the preferred type for many
express operators, was the allotted mount of Driver Eric L. Jones
from May 1930: 'It was a good coach, and it would go and go.
It was nothing to drive up to London from Bournemouth, and
on one's return to find Johnny Elliott waiting for you. He'd say
"Laddie, go and have a cup of tea and a sandwich and then pop
off to Plymouth", which meant that from an early morning shift
you'd find yourself working right through to 9 o'clock the
following morning.' However, the Tiger was later relegated to
the Newport, Isle of Wight, garage, whence it was eventually
rescued by Hants & Dorset.

Hants & Dorset's bus station at The Square, Bournemouth,
opened for business on Sunday 8 March 1931. The ticket office
and the coach station on the lower floor were leased, as arranged,

Towards the end of the 1929 season, Elliott Bros ordered single examples of four chassis from competing manufacturers, in order to decide future purchasing policy. All four were fitted with reinforced bodywork designed and built by Duple. The competitors were an AEC Regal, a Daimler CF6, a Leyland Tiger and this Maudslay ML6, LJ 651, seen later at St Mawes as Western National No 3621.
Alan Lambert collection

As a result of the trials, Elliott Bros chose to stay with AEC and Daimler. It liked the 'crash-proof' bodywork by Duple, however, and this featured upon deliveries of both types of chassis until the last in July 1930. LJ 652 was the trial Daimler CF6 of the quartet, and was the prototype for 15 further CF6s received in this guise — the last Daimlers to serve with Elliott Bros.
Peter Delaney collection

A popular type of A.E.C. "Regal" Royal Blue long distance Coach.

The Associated Equipment Co., Ltd., Southall, Middx.
BUILDERS OF LONDON'S BUSES

to Elliott Bros. Since there was sufficient room for the overnight parking of up to 20 coaches, Royal Blue promptly moved its express operations headquarters there from Holdenhurst Road. Throughout Hants & Dorset's operational portion of the building, the rubber floors and the decor were green; Royal Blue's part was similarly finished in blue, whilst above its entrance the neon-lit lettering included the words 'Royal Blue Automobile Services'. Coaches entered the lower-floor station anti-clockwise in order to bring their passenger doors alongside the centrally-located platforms at this level. At night and high above, one of the two tall masts atop the façade carried at its head a bright blue lamp. Whether by day or by night, when the interior was a blaze of light, it was spectacular and passers-by stopped to stare as coaches were seen 'zooming in and out like bees about a hive'.

At the time of the station's out-of-season opening, there were 18 express arrivals and departures each day, including seven for London. By the summer there were 23, with considerable multiplication by relief vehicles. The 'inspectors', as the Elliotts called their conductors, reported to a station superintendent. Each inspector was responsible for all duplicate coaches on any one route, and all charting from sub-agents and offices was carried out at the new station from the outset.

Only express services used the Royal Blue coach station. Tours and excursions continued, until the 1935 season, to depart from the southeast corner of The Square. Since the local authority had approved the building of the bus station in order to relieve congestion at that location, it is curious that it then proceeded to grant licences to tour operators additional to Royal Blue's established competitors. Among the newcomers was Highways (Bournemouth) Ltd, set up by its parent company to tap local tours and excursions traffic. Its Gilford 168OT-type 26-seater coach (GJ 8373) was frequently parked at the head of the stand, very close to the entrance of the new station. Elliott Bros was

stung into action and attempted to purchase the undertaking. However, Tillings stepped in and made a better offer on behalf of its Western National and Southern National subsidiaries. In doing so, it gave the National companies their first foothold in Bournemouth — which would have momentous consequences for Royal Blue, just over a season later.

The Elliotts had better luck with Traveller Saloon Coaches Ltd of Plymouth, whose two-year-old Plymouth-Portsmouth express service and Southsea-Bristol route (acquired from Olympic Motor Services Ltd in 1932) were transferred to Royal Blue in July 1933. The vehicles included in that purchase were three Gilfords, two Chevrolets and a Dennis Lancet, all of which entered the Royal Blue fleet.

Elliott Bros now had 106 modern coaches in service, none more than five years old. Unfortunately this expenditure had been encouraged by a yearly-increasing traffic which now stopped in its tracks. The 'Great Depression', with over three

million in Britain unemployed by 1933, caused a considerable drop in the number of people who could afford to travel for pleasure. Stage-carriage operators like Hants & Dorset suffered reductions in income of over 20%. No figure for Royal Blue survives but, clearly, for independents reliant upon tours and express work, the position was much worse. The Elliotts attempted to cut costs to the bone, considered becoming a public rather than a private company, and had inconclusive takeover discussions with the Red & White group, then in the midst of expanding its operations because of its stronger capital base.

Red & White Services Ltd and Elliott Bros (Bournemouth) Ltd were already among six operators discussing the formation of a co-ordination scheme designed to avoid unnecessary and competitive duplication of express services on a network centred upon Cheltenham, where Black & White Motorways' General Manager H. R. Lapper chaired the meetings. This came to fruition on 1 July 1934 as 'Associated Motorways', with Greyhound Motor Services, Midland Red and United Counties as the three other founding members of the scheme. The transfer of seven Royal Blue routes to Associated Motorways control represented a welcome saving, as revenue allocated upon a mileage-run basis gained unprecedented economies. Associated Motorways did not operate its own vehicles, although, to avoid favouritism, it adopted the image of a lurid orange and green coach upon its publicity and timetables. Royal Blue and its fellow operators continued to ply upon their allotted routes in their traditional liveries. Services not included in the scheme remained the business of those operators (granted the necessary licences) already established along such roads.

The Elliotts' last — and successful — attempt to upstage their rivals came following an order for four of AEC's revolutionary 'Q' chassis, with engine mounted below floor level on the offside behind the front axle, which was itself set back from the front of the vehicle. The first of the type to be fitted with a coach body, LJ 8001, was delivered to Royal Blue in August 1933 and was a head-turner from the start. The full-fronted bodywork by Duple would not have been

Hants & Dorset's bus station at The Square, Bournemouth, designed by local architects Jackson & Greenen, opened in March 1931. The lower floor was leased to Elliott Bros as a coach station for express workings. *Above* is the architects' original design for the lower-floor coach station, and *below* that eventually constructed and brought into use. The original concept appears to have been drafted in the days of normal-control coaches.
Colin Morris collection

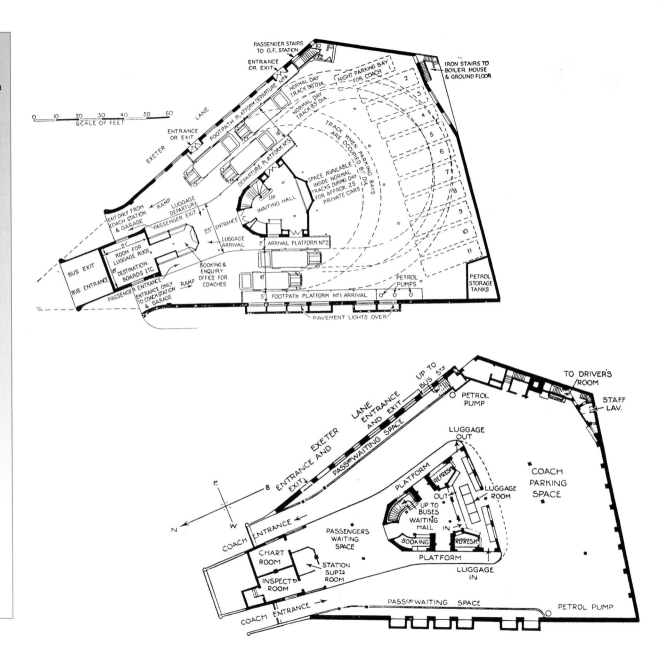

38

noticeably out of fashion some 60 years later. The following winter, this coach was joined by two others by the same coachbuilder, one featuring a higher floor-line to allow all seats to face forward. The last of the quartet was AEL 2, bodied by Harrington of Hove and delivered in June 1934. Each was used upon express service duties, and a rush to board one ensued if it appeared in a line of Royal Blue coaches. All four caused a similar rush when they appeared upon the excursions stand in The Square.

Harrington painted at least one additional Q in Royal Blue colours and used it as a demonstrator, and possibly produced a similarly-painted semi-observation-style body upon an AEC Regal tried out by Elliott Bros. However, references to a mysterious coach (AEL 495) have proved to be an erroneous reading of the registration records: this vehicle was a Leyland Beaver TSC8 drop-side lorry delivered to another 'Elliott Bros' — proprietors of a brick- and drainpipe-manufacturing business with premises in Bear Cross and at West Howe Pottery.

Two Royal Blue coaches (LJ 8001 and LJ 8600) were hired in 1934 by the British Photographic Fellowship, which travelled from London through France, Germany and Austria, the vehicles crossing from Dover to Calais aboard Townsend's ferry *Forde*. This much-photographed journey provided considerable publicity for AEC, Duple and, of course, Elliott Bros, but, for the latter, came too late.

The new regulations introduced in 1931, which required permission for every journey beforehand and regular re-application for existing services, produced a 'swings and roundabouts' situation: in 1932, the Traffic Commissioners had refused permission for Royal Blue to go further east than Portsmouth on the South Coast route which it had pioneered. Such 'red tape' had caused the Elliotts (like their counterpart, Chapman of Eastbourne) to tire somewhat of the whole business, and they became receptive to an attractive takeover bid.

Prompted by the observant Southern National, Thomas Tilling Ltd, already a London agent for Royal Blue at Peckham, entered into negotiations with Elliott Bros during the autumn of 1934; these led to an agreement, effective from 1 January 1935, for the sale, for the sum of £122,500, of the goodwill, vehicles and other property of Elliott Bros (Bournemouth) Ltd, which assets to be divided, more-or-less equally, between the Tilling subsidiaries Southern National, Western National and Hants & Dorset. The Elliott brothers thus withdrew from the coach and car-hire industry but, surprisingly, the firm of Elliott Bros (Bournemouth) Ltd was not finally wound up until 15 June 1939.

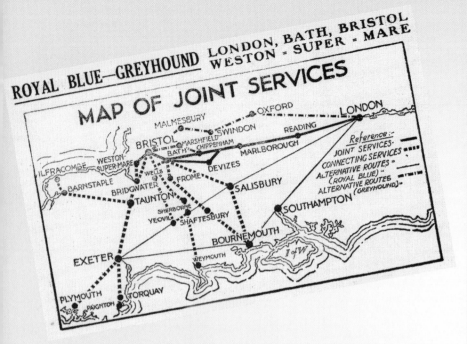

ROYAL BLUE—GREYHOUND LONDON, BATH, BRISTOL WESTON-SUPER-MARE

MAP OF JOINT SERVICES

Reference:—
JOINT SERVICES
CONNECTING SERVICES
ALTERNATIVE ROUTES (ROYAL BLUE)
ALTERNATIVE ROUTES (GREYHOUND)

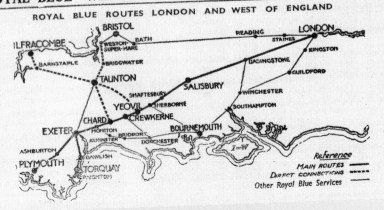

ROYAL BLUE—WESTERN NATIONAL—SOUTHERN NATIONAL

ROYAL BLUE ROUTES LONDON AND WEST OF ENGLAND

Reference
MAIN ROUTES
DIRECT CONNECTIONS
Other Royal Blue Services

1932 Summer Service — Commencing May 9th

The Symbol of Safety

Royal Blue Automobile Services

In conjunction with the

| SOUTHDOWN MOTOR SERVICES | EAST KENT ROAD CAR CO, LTD. |

Route B. Table 6

Hastings, Eastbourne,

Brighton, Portsmouth, Torquay,

Plymouth, And all SOUTH DEVON

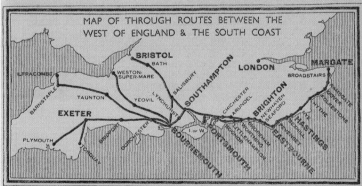

MAP OF THROUGH ROUTES BETWEEN THE WEST OF ENGLAND & THE SOUTH COAST

Through services are maintained daily—winter and summer—at varying departure times connecting the Southdown and East Kent Companies systems in the South and East with the Royal Blue Automobile Services to Bournemouth and the West of England.

ELLIOTT BROS. (BMTH) LIMITED
—68-70 HOLDENHURST ROAD—
BOURNEMOUTH   PHONE 6262

SOUTHDOWN MOTOR SERVICES
5 STEINE STREET   LIMITED
BRIGHTON   TELEPHONE 4033

10,000 13/6/32

Elliott Bros' *Royal Blue Weekly* was a remarkable publication which grew into a 20-page booklet. It listed the guaranteed tours for the forthcoming week, 'topics of interest' — right down to which ships would be visiting Southampton (that week, the *Carinthia*, *Homeric* and *Empress of Australia*), detailed descriptions of tours, maps, express service timetables, and a proud description of its new type of coach. *Colin Billington collection*

In July 1933, Elliott Bros purchased the licences and six vehicles of Traveller Saloon Coaches Ltd of Princes Square, Plymouth. One year earlier, that firm had acquired the business of Olympic Motor Services Ltd of Southsea, Hampshire. This Gilford 168OT with Weymann coachwork (either TP 9181 or TP 9182) thus served in all three fleets before being acquired by Tilling in 1935 and sent its separate way.
Alan Lambert collection

Way ahead of its time, the remarkable Q-type chassis was produced by AEC. The first fitted with coach bodywork (by Duple) was received by Elliott Bros at Bournemouth in August 1933. Royal Blue's Manager, Harry Rollings, described it as 'like something out of another world', and he wasn't far wrong. A comparison with the Regal and its 'crash-proof' body, of just three years earlier, gives an illustration of what he meant.
Ian Allan Library

Elliott Bros operated a total of four AEC Q coaches. The second (LJ 8600, seen together with LJ 8001) was delivered in November 1933. The coachwork was again by Duple, although of a revised design. Both were originally 35-seaters, with luggage-racks fitted opposite the entrance door, although LJ 8600 was without the roof pannier for the internal storage of suitcases, as designed by Duple for LJ 8001.
Philip Davies collection

Built as a speculative venture by a local builder, the garage, offices and café at 8 Bath Road were occupied on a leasehold basis by Elliott Bros, which named it the 'Pavilion Garage'. It passed to Hants & Dorset in 1935, and at one stage became the registered office of that company. Beside it is AEL 2 of June 1934, the fourth Q, bearing a 35-seat Harrington semi-observation body in two-tone blue.
Colin Morris collection

The third Royal Blue Q (LJ 8601), received in March 1934 and again bodied by Duple, earned itself the nickname 'Jumbo' because of its tall front profile and higher bodyline. This was brought about by a raised floor level, in order to provide an additional two seats over the engine which, in the Q, was set on the offside, behind the front wheel. In the first, as originally constructed, the luggage-rack occupied the position directly above the power unit.
Philip Davies collection

44

In the summer of 1934, LJ 8001 and LJ 8600 conveyed members of the British Photographic Fellowship from England to Austria. The passage across the English Channel was made aboard the Townsend ferry *Forde* (registered in Hull) from Dover to Calais. LJ 8001 is being hoisted aboard *(above left)*, and being refuelled in France *(above)* at a Standard Oil (Esso) service station. Even the Q-type was still petrol-engined. *Philip Davies collection*

A report in a journal suggested that a fifth Q coach was at the point of being acquired when Thomas Tilling Ltd negotiated the purchase of Royal Blue in late 1934. That would explain this picture of an unregistered Harrington-bodied example which, ironically, subsequently served with Walter Maitland's 'Excelsior' fleet at Bournemouth. Before that, there had been another Q in Royal Blue livery (actually registered LJ 8601 originally) which went elsewhere. *Philip Davies collection*

Upon acquisition by Thomas Tilling Ltd in January 1935, the express work of Royal Blue was transferred to Western and Southern National. Those vehicles acquired by them were at first pressed into service in Elliott Bros' livery. Thus RU 8807, one of the AEC Reliance/Duple coaches with 'sunshine roof' configuration has become Southern National No 3712, although it still carries the as yet unremoved Elliott Bros garter upon its flanks.
Cheltenham Bus Preservation Group

4. Tilling's Royal Blue

Thomas Tilling Ltd decreed that the express coach business developed by Elliott Bros (Bournemouth) Ltd should become the preserve of the Western National and Southern National companies, based at Queen Street, Exeter. Since virtually all the tours and excursions, plus private-hire work, of Royal Blue was based upon Bournemouth, headquarters also of Tilling-controlled Hants & Dorset Motor Services Ltd, the latter firm was chosen to acquire this section as a going concern.

Until the 1933 season, the National companies' express services had been operated during the summer months only. So, with just two years' experience of regular activity in that field to their credit, Western and Southern National found themselves in charge of a greatly-increased network of regular and seasonal long-distance services. The two managements had prepared for this for several months before the takeover, when express traffic

to the West Country had been co-ordinated with Elliott Bros upon a percentage basis not dissimilar to that employed by Associated Motorways.

The Exeter-based companies were fortunate to secure the services of the Elliotts' Traffic Manager, Clem Preece, a man well versed in the proceedings relating to this specialised aspect of the industry, the traffic courts, and dealings with and on behalf of Associated Motorways. The acquisition of Royal Blue's express services made the National companies members of that association for the first time. Preece, who now became Traffic Superintendent (Express Services) for his new employers, had learned the basics of express operation with Kingston & Modern Travel Ltd, of Southampton. He had transferred to Capt Reginald Keevil's 'Holland Motor Coaches' (also of Southampton) in 1928, before being appointed by the Elliotts at Bournemouth in

January 1930. Although Preece was based in Exeter, the main hub of Royal Blue operations (which name and basic livery the National companies decided to retain for all their express work) remained at Bournemouth.

The National express routes from London to the West Country, which now took on the Royal Blue identity, included those to Swanage and Weymouth (Dorset) and Lynton and Ilfracombe (Devon). The inclusion of the National routes to Bude, and to St Ives and Penzance, took 'Royal Blue' express services into Cornwall for the first time; this county was not part of the Associated Motorways network.

Ex-Elliott Bros properties accruing to National included the booking office at 11 Prince Street, Bristol (held briefly), small leased properties in Torquay and Paignton, and the three freehold buildings which comprised the engineering shop and two garages at Rutland Road, Bournemouth — one allotted to Western National, the other to Southern National. The National companies were to pay Hants & Dorset £2,000 per annum for the rent of the Bournemouth coach station, and one third of the rates of the whole building. Of the Elliott vehicles, Western National received nine ADC 424s, two ADC 426s, eight AEC Reliances, six Daimler CF6s, seven AEC Regals and one each of Chevrolet, Dennis, Gilford and Maudslay manufacture (36 vehicles). Southern National was allotted nine ADC 424s, two ADC 426s, eight AEC Reliances, eight Daimler CF6s, six AEC Regals, one Chevrolet and one Gilford (35). To keep the wheels turning without disruption, the National companies employed a large proportion of Elliott staff with appropriate experience.

Not surprisingly, Hants & Dorset's one third share of the purchase price was £40,833 6s 8d (£40,833.33 approximately — which goes to show how much neater pounds, shillings and pence used to be!). For that, this company received the goodwill of the Elliotts' tours, excursions and private-hire business, the right to the title 'Royal Blue — Bournemouth', the hire-car department, and the relevant staff led by Elliott Bros' General Manager Harry Rollings, who would become 'Manager, Tours & Excursions'. Also included were the freehold of Yarmouth garage, Isle of Wight, and the leaseholds of the following properties: garage and office, 68 Holdenhurst Road and shop at 70 Holdenhurst Road, shops at 3 Richmond Hill, 93B St Michael's Road, and the Pavilion Garage, offices and restaurant at 8 Bath Road (all in Bournemouth), plus a shop at 881 Christchurch Road and an office at the Savoy Picture House, Boscombe. In addition, Hants & Dorset acquired eight ADC

424s, two ADC 426s, nine AEC Reliances, seven Daimler CF6s, six AEC Regals, all four AEC Qs, one Gilford and that one Leyland Tiger coach languishing on the Isle of Wight (38 vehicles).

Although George Cardwell of Tilling is credited with deciding how many vehicles of each type the three companies should receive, Harry Rollings was quite adamant (when interviewed in 1957) that it was he who decided exactly which ones within those categories would go with him to Hants & Dorset, and made particularly sure that he got the ultra-modern AEC Qs. Whilst the National companies numbered and, in one way or another, found employment for all the Elliott vehicles allotted to them, Hants & Dorset's engineering department was remarkably choosy. Six ADC 424, both ADC 426 and all nine AEC Reliance coaches

Elliott Bros' tours and excursions were passed by Tilling to Hants & Dorset Motor Services Ltd, at the time based at the Royal Mews, Bournemouth. This company did not employ the AEC Reliance and Gilford coaches it acquired, and only two of the ADC 424 type were used temporarily. Instead, in time for the start of the 1935 season, it had 14 specially-prepared Leyland Tiger TS7 coaches with Beadle bodywork delivered, dressed in a livery of dark blue and turquoise. *Colin Morris collection*

Also in 1935, Tilling acquired Tourist Motor Coaches (Southampton) Ltd, the express services again going to the National companies and the tours to Hants & Dorset. The Tourist fleet, in a livery of two-tone blue and cream, comprised largely Albions and Leyland Tiger coaches, with bodywork by Strachans. This unidentified Tiger TS3 model has the latter-day reinforced lower panels incorporating dished opening lockers for carrying extra luggage. *Philip Davies collection*

Tourist itself made acquisitions, including Aloysius Browne's 'Hiawatha & Queen'. Browne had launched his business as 'Queen Motor Coaches', based in Bitterne Park, and acquired 'Hiawatha' in 1922. He had already started a service from Southampton to London on a regular basis, with two pneumatic-tyred Crossley charabancs with cape-cart hoods. CR 6722 is pictured after that amalgamation, on a private-hire trip to Bournemouth Pier.
Alan Lambert collection

were put up for sale immediately. They were replaced in time for the 1935 touring season by 14 brand-new Leyland Tiger TS7 coaches with streamlined semi-observation-style coachwork by Beadle — clearly designed and ordered by Hants & Dorset well before the dust of takeover negotiations had settled.

A similar division of assets took place when the express, tours and excursions business of Tourist Coaches (Southampton) Ltd was acquired in July 1935, although news of this Tilling takeover was actually announced before that of the Elliotts' Royal Blue. Tourist had been founded by Bertie H. Ransom at Back-of-the-Walls, Southampton, with a pair of GMC charabancs, followed by several Karriers. In February 1923, he acquired the Vivid Motor Touring Co's three AEC charabancs, and moved his head office to 171 St Mary's Road. The General Strike in 1926 gave him the opportunity to run ships' passengers to London — the start of his express work. Ransom joined forces in 1927 with S. C. Bullock and Thomas Briggs, who had sold their transport

interests in Lancashire to Ribble and come south to start afresh. However, they first purchased W. Aloysius Browne's 'Hiawatha Motor Coaches', together with his base in Winchester Road. Browne had started in 1919 and was an early provider of transport between Southampton and London with his 'Queen Motor Coaches' garaged at Bitterne Park. He had bought the two vehicles and goodwill of 'Hiawatha Coaches' in 1922, and re-styled his business 'Hiawatha & Queen', with an office at Six Dials and an additional garage near the West station. By July 1923, his fleet, at eight coaches, was the same size as Ransom's; both at the time claimed to be 'the largest in Southampton' — an interesting comparison with the excursions and tours potential of Bournemouth at that time.

Tourist Motor Coaches (Southampton) Ltd had been formed on 1 November 1927. It rebuilt the garage facilities in Winchester Road and opened 'The Tourist Motor Station' in Grosvenor Square. The revitalised firm captured most of the local tours work,

When Tilling took over Tourist, the same dark blue and turquoise colours were applied to those coaches acquired by Hants & Dorset, but with the identity 'Tourist — Southampton'. After the second touring season, Hants & Dorset decided to dispense with the overtly 'Royal Blue' and 'Tourist' identities. F564 (CEL 229) wears Tilling green and cream with 'Royal Blue & Tourist' enclosed in an H&D garter; this lasted until 1946.
Colin Morris collection

extended its express activity westward to Bournemouth and Plymouth, and established a port-to-port service on three days per week between Southampton and Liverpool, running via Oxford and Stratford-upon-Avon. By the autumn of 1933 it was operating a fleet of five Chevrolets, 18 Leylands, 12 Albions and three Studebaker coaches, at which time the board purchased Major James Jackson's 'Coliseum Coaches' based at the Savoy Hotel, Above Bar and the Devon Hotel, Queen's Terrace. That added a Lancia, three Maudslays, an Albion, an AEC (plus a Daimler taxi) to the Tourist fleet, and secured the services of Jackson in a managerial role.

Upon acquisition by Tilling, the Tourist directors retired from the profession, but the firm's Secretary, Lee Fletcher, was appointed Western National's 'Traffic Superintendent, Royal Blue' at Bournemouth, and Jackson became 'Tours Manager, Southampton' for Hants & Dorset. Southern National acquired the premises at Six Dials and, briefly, title to the freehold Grosvenor Square/Bedford Place site, which it sold to Hants & Dorset for £25,000, and title of Torrington Lodge and the garage, Winchester Road, sold to Hants & Dorset for £7,882; the documents were sealed in June 1935. Of the vehicles, Western National received two Chevrolet, one Studebaker, five Albion, two Leyland and two Maudslay coaches (12 vehicles). Southern National was allotted one Chevrolet, three Albion, four Leyland, an AEC, a Lancia, a Maudslay (11 coaches), and the Daimler taxi.

Hants & Dorset received 10 Leylands and Jackson's little Albion Victor 20-seat coach, for which 11 coaches it paid Southern National £4,972, plus 15s (75p) in the pound for 12 months as goodwill in respect of receipts from excursions, tours and contract carriages at Southampton — estimated at over £9,000. It also received the right to the title 'Tourist — Southampton'.

For two seasons, Hants & Dorset operated its Royal Blue and Tourist coaches — and its new ones delivered during that period — in a dark blue and turquoise livery. From 1937 it decided instead to adopt Tilling green and cream (with a touch of BET dark green) colours, although Hants & Dorset coaches continued to display the words 'Royal Blue & Tourist' within a garter device until 1946. Of the Tourist vehicles which went to the National companies, the larger ones were pressed into Royal Blue service, which name was then extended to the ex-Tourist express services, but only two Leyland Tigers and the AEC Regal were retained at length in that role.

As soon as the National companies realised that their express operations were to be thus greatly enlarged, they ordered for their new Royal Blue fleet 28 Bristol JJW chassis, to be divided equally between the two. Since time was of the essence, the task of building the 32-seat bodywork went to three firms: Beadle, Eastern Counties and Weymann (MCW). It was built to a National specification, based upon existing saloon buses, but featured a streamlined pannier upon the rear roof, together with luxurious fittings throughout the vehicle. The type became a Royal Blue standard until World War 2, and was employed also to rebody some earlier vehicles. It was applied to 10 ex-Devon General Leyland Tiger coaches in 1936 and to two more from Silver Cars of Seaton in 1937, which also entered service with Royal Blue. That same year, a further 16 similar bodies were applied to new AEC Regal chassis, eight, from Mumford, for Western National and the rest, from Duple, for Southern National. Together with 20 ex-Elliott, 11 ex-National and three ex-Tourist rebodied coaches, there were 88 vehicles on the road in this standard Royal Blue style by the outbreak of World War 2.

Western National had gained control of Bristol Tramways & Carriage Co's finances and was thus able to forge closer links between Royal Blue and Greyhound. Both National companies introduced 'Royal Blue express plus holiday breaks' in conjunction with their existing tours and excursion centres in the South West, and four non-stop services from London: 'Channel Coast Express' (to Bournemouth), 'Cornish Coast Express' (Penzance), 'Minehead Express' and the 'Weymouth Bay Express'. The National companies also set up a Royal Blue outstation — always considered a subsidiary of Bournemouth depot — at the Hilsea and Portsmouth garages of Southdown Motor Services Ltd. This provided 'first and last' facilities to and from the west and its vehicles went east from there 'on hire' to Southdown and East Kent as far as Margate, along roads once familiar to Elliott Bros. A completely new express service, Bristol-Glastonbury-Bridport, was introduced, and feeder services to the main Royal Blue routes were begun in Cornwall as part of a scheme which would provide 'Royal Blue' connections for all those strikingly picturesque destinations in the West Country. There was also a brief flirtation with air travel: the London-Bournemouth service offered connections at Southampton's Eastleigh airport with flights to the Isle of Wight provided by the Monospar aircraft of the Portsmouth, Southsea & IoW Aviation Co Ltd — an arrangement brought to a premature end by the outbreak of another war with Germany.

It is possible that the dark blue
and turquoise livery was a
Tilling directive (a mixture of
dark blue, Tilling green and
cream, for the latter ?), because
some of the new vehicles
ordered for Western and
Southern National express-
service use also wore it briefly,
albeit in a different layout.
These were Bristol JJW
coaches bodied by Eastern
Counties, Beadle and MCW.
Within the eight bodied by
Eastern Counties, several
livery trials were evident.
ECW Archive/
S. J. Butler collection

In the first of the livery
experiments, No 163
(BTA 453) had the 'Royal
Blue' fleetname displayed
upon turquoise flanks with
fleetnumbers encircled by
'Western National' in a garter
without buckle. No 164
(BTA 454) for Southern
National had a lighter turquoise
roof with company name
around a winged and dust-
trailed wheel and large initial
'N'. It was this fleetname
device which was adopted as
standard, together with the
reduced beading of No 164.
ECW Archive/
S. J. Butler collection

No 167 (BTA 497) had another variation with no sign of ultramarine, the dark blue with cream stripe not being enhanced by a Bristol peculiarity of the time — an unpainted, polished bonnet-cover. All three, together with others of the batch and subsequent deliveries, had black wings. The linen screens above the side windows usually showed company or Royal Blue identity phrases, but occasionally displayed route details.
Bristol Vintage Bus Group

Whereas Hants & Dorset immediately placed its acquired ADC 426/AEC Reliance coaches on sale, the National companies had 10 of them rebodied by Beadle at the end of the 1935 season. Because of the chassis length, the new bodies were a shortened version of the standard Royal Blue pattern, with seats for only 28 passengers. No 3712 (RU 8807) of Southern National is parked in front of full-size Leyland Tiger No 41 (DR 8806).
Philip Davies collection

The second batch of Bristol JJW coaches — 10 bodied by Beadle and 10 by MCW — were divided equally between Western and Southern National. No 177 (ATT 927) wears the eventual livery chosen for this style of body, and is pictured post-World War 2 in the company of Midland Red CHA 983, which firm ran jointly with Royal Blue, for Associated Motorways, between Portsmouth and Birmingham. *Omnibus Society*

Originally a Duple-bodied coach of Southern National, No 3104 (YD 2307), a Leyland Tiger TS1 of 1931, was fitted with a Covrad replacement radiator (considered more modern) and rebodied for Royal Blue service by Beadle in May 1939. Like the other 10 Tigers transferred from the Western and Southern National fleets during the late 'thirties, it retained its original 'bonnet-number' identity in Royal Blue livery. *Alan Cross*

▲ In 1937 the National companies followed Elliott Bros' example of seven years previously and ordered AEC Regal chassis for Royal Blue. Eight for Western National were bodied by the local Devon firm, Mumford, and eight for Southern National by Duple to the same design. No 1062 (ETA 996) represents the last batch built to this pattern on a new chassis. Fifteen were rebodied by Beadle in 1949 for continued Royal Blue service. *Peter Delaney collection*

Of the 12 ex-Elliott AEC Regal coaches transferred to the National companies (six went to Hants & Dorset for tours and excursions work), five were allotted to Southern National. No 3731 (LJ 1525) was one of these, and was rebodied by Beadle in 1935, hence the rear entrance. From 1937 onwards a front entrance, which incidentally permitted a streamlined taper on the rear wing, was preferred. *Philip Davies collection*

Posing on Dartmoor in one of the 'deep valleys' which gave Devon its name is No 3631 (LJ 1519) — one of several publicity pictures taken of the vehicle in 1939. The blind as set shows a conflicting route between London and Plymouth. The vehicle was one of seven AEC Regals from Elliott Bros operated by Western National and was rebodied in this style by Beadle that year. Sadly, this coach was damaged beyond repair by the Luftwaffe in 1943. *Ian Allan Library*

The personnel, buildings and vehicles of Western and Southern National suffered greatly during World War 2. There was a great deal of hastily-arranged rushing back and forth in the newly-imposed blackout during September 1939 before, in what became known as 'The Phoney War', it was realised that not too much enemy activity was actually taking place. There were numerous additional journeys provided to take London school evacuees to the West Country, visits to them by anxious parents, and a partial drift back to their homes before winter. In the midst of all this, Royal Blue coaches were commandeered to take part in troop-movement exercises, whilst others were converted into ambulances for Admiralty use.

In the South West of England, isolated Luftwaffe sorties commenced in June 1940, gradually becoming more severe. Given that National employees lost their lives, and many more were injured, it may seem invidious to say that, despite severe damage to company property at Weymouth (October 1940) and Plymouth (March 1941, April 1941 and April 1944), only two coaches in Royal Blue livery were damaged (and later repaired), in the first of the Plymouth incidents. There was a narrow escape for the Rutland Road premises in Bournemouth, part of which had been requisitioned for war work, and the Six Dials offices were rendered unsuitable for further use during one of the many raids upon Southampton.

At the outbreak of World War 2, Royal Blue coaches were earmarked to perform numerous additional duties, including the transportation of evacuee children, as ambulances and troop transports. Troops of the Devonshire Regiment are on manoeuvres with some of the 10 ex-Devon General Leyland Tigers set aside for that purpose. The latter had been rebodied to Royal Blue standard by Beadle in 1936. *Colin Billington collection*

The suspension of express services in World War 2 saw Royal Blue coaches pressed into service as stage-carriage buses at various points in the Western and Southern National companies' joint system. Latterly, several Leyland and Bristol coaches were fitted with Tilling T2-type gas trailers, built by Bristol and burning anthracite, in an effort to save precious petrol. Bristol JJW No 179 (ATT 929) displays the linkage fitting. *Omnibus Society*

Two Mumford-bodied AEC Regals of 1937 (Nos 1053 and 1056) and Beadle-bodied ex-Tourist Leyland Tiger No 3537 await passengers for Southampton and Bournemouth at Victoria Coach Station. It is the first winter of World War 2; the vehicles feature white wing-tips and dumb-irons and the early form of masked headlights. At least six passengers are carrying respirators (gas masks). *Colin Morris collection*

Not surprisingly, the greatest continual pressure upon Royal Blue staff was at the Victoria Coach Station, London, sub-depot, who were under constant bombardment, and 19 coaches were damaged by incendiaries and shell splinters. Driving a Royal Blue coach into Plymouth, Southampton or London after dark was not something for the faint-hearted. The Tilling group's booklet *The War that Went on Wheels* recorded the experience of a Royal Blue driver attempting to reach Victoria with the 3.30pm from Bournemouth in November 1940. After he had passed through Kingston,

'Anti-aircraft guns began firing from unseen positions near the road and mingled with their firing were the explosions of falling bombs. I thought the only thing to do was keep going and trust to luck. I was actually on Putney Heath when it happened — one terrific explosion and the coach seemed to shoot away from underneath me. I felt as though I was flying through the air with the coach. I clung on to the steering wheel, although this did not stop me from being severely bumped around inside the cab. I remember wondering what had happened and then saw I was rushing towards some trees. The coach swerved and hit a wall and fence. My first thought was what had happened to my passengers? They were shaken, but uninjured. I went back to find the cause of the trouble — there was a great crater nearly covering the road where I had passed a second before.'

He spoke afterwards of the courage of his passengers on wild journeys of this kind, who, if asked if they wished to take cover, nearly always gave the same answer: 'We leave it to you, Driver — get through if you can.'

Southern National's 1062 (ETA 996) caught fire at Tidworth in 1939 and, in so doing, set the trend for the future design of a large proportion of Royal Blue's fleet a decade later. Its chassis was rebodied in April 1941 with this streamlined 31-seater coachwork by Duple. Based upon that firm's *avant garde* design which, but for the war, would have become its standard, it created a big impression. *Ian Allan Library*

Much impressed, Southern National received a second example of Duple's advanced product in June 1941. This was also a rebodied AEC Regal, but a vehicle with a rather more chequered history. No 3540 (OW 3167) had been new in 1933 to James Jackson's Coliseum Coaches of Southampton, fitted with a Harrington body. It had been acquired by Tourist soon after, and was transferred to Southern National in May 1935. *P. Yeomans collection*

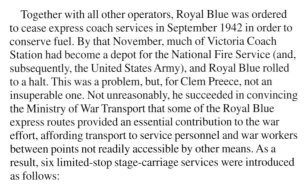

Together with all other operators, Royal Blue was ordered to cease express coach services in September 1942 in order to conserve fuel. By that November, much of Victoria Coach Station had become a depot for the National Fire Service (and, subsequently, the United States Army), and Royal Blue rolled to a halt. This was a problem, but, for Clem Preece, not an insuperable one. Not unreasonably, he succeeded in convincing the Ministry of War Transport that some of the Royal Blue express routes provided an essential contribution to the war effort, affording transport to service personnel and war workers between points not readily accessible by other means. As a result, six limited-stop stage-carriage services were introduced as follows:

400	Bournemouth-New Milton-Southampton
401	Southampton-Fareham-Portsmouth
402	Bournemouth-Bridport-Exeter
403	Bournemouth-Sherborne-Yeovil
404	Honiton-Yeovil-Shaftesbury
405	Bournemouth-Shaftesbury-Trowbridge

Some two dozen coaches were maintained to work these routes in rotation, not normally more than two on any one service, and this succeeded in keeping the Royal Blue flag flying at the very least. Many of the remainder were relegated to running as comparatively unromantic stage-carriage buses at various locations in National territory. Some, based upon Taunton particularly, were propelled by producer gas in that role, in an attempt to save even more precious petrol.

Even the Royal Blue name itself supported the war effort. At least one fortified pill-box, protecting the western approaches to Portsmouth — at Ranvilles Lane, Titchfield — carried in large letters the legend 'Royal Blue Booking Office', something of a disappointment for any intending passenger who looked inside. Probably the last damage inflicted by the Luftwaffe upon Royal Blue occurred in Park Gate, near Southampton, when, in the early hours of Whit Monday, 1944, a lone bomb destroyed six French-Canadian tanks awaiting the call to D-Day. As they burned, they peppered the area with 100mm shells, one going clean through the Royal Blue timetable-case nearby.

Post-World War 2, Royal Blue express services recommenced as far west as Plymouth in April 1946, and on into Cornwall that June. By winter, even the South Coast Express was going as far east as Hastings, courtesy of Southdown from Portsmouth. Since — apart from some rebodying — no replacement vehicles had

been delivered during the war, the resumption involved some Herculean effort in the workshops to gird up the existing Royal Blue fleet. Vehicle replacement recommenced in May 1948 with the arrival of the first of 45 Bristol L coaches with 31-seat coachwork, delivered between then and October 1949 — 10 with AEC engines (L6A) and all the rest with the newly-developed lightweight six-cylinder Bristol Tramways-built unit (L6B). The crackling roar of an L6B engine-start in the depths of Bournemouth Coach Station rivalled anything heard in the pits at Silverstone race circuit.

The coachwork of the new Bristols was impressive too, having been based upon a late-'thirties Duple design already in service with Western and Southern National, but built under licence by Beadle. Retained were the sloping pillars and streamlined body lines, a departure from the strictly horizontal stretchers of previous (and subsequent) Royal Blue bodywork designs. Also employed were staggered seats and the streamlined roof pannier, for many years a feature of Royal Blue coaches. All 15 remaining members of the 1937 batch of AEC Regals were rebodied in the same style by Beadle in the spring of 1949. Duple Motor Bodies Ltd was itself able to provide near-identical 33-seat coachwork for 10 L6B models delivered in 1950, and for 15 longer 37-seat LL6B examples purchased in 1951, following new regulations permitting single-deck buses to be 30ft in length.

The Beadle-bodied Bristols had arrived in time to take part in traffic created by a postwar populace anxious to travel to beautiful locations both cheaply and in some style. How pleasant, to roll through country towns and villages with a relatively high viewpoint, to watch the world go by! This was much better than the 'back yard' look of towns viewed from the railway lines, and, until 1950, when petrol rationing was at last ended, there were few private cars on the road to slow the progress of the coach. Up hill, down dale and around the corner in a luxurious coach — for the young, at least, the journey was the best part of the holiday. Perhaps these were the real 'glory days' of Royal Blue?

In 1948, a change of little immediate consequence to Royal Blue's contented passengers had taken place. Clement Attlee's Labour Government, bent upon the nationalisation of Britain's transport, and having already brought the railways into public ownership, succeeded in convincing Thomas Tilling Ltd and its shareholders to sell their interests in buses to the British Transport Commission. It was arranged, however, that each company should retain its local title and management. Re-titled the Tilling Association Ltd, the existing board of directors was to

After a gap of over 10 years, Royal Blue received new vehicles again with effect from May 1948. The chassis was the postwar version of the Bristol L, and over the next two and a half years, 45 with Bristol engines and 10 with AEC units were delivered. Bodywork was based upon Duple's earlier design, but was 'cleaned up' by P. R. Irlam, Chief Designer at Beadle, which firm built all save the last 10. No 1205 (JUO 937), of the first batch, is at Broadclyst, Devon.
Calton Phoenix collection

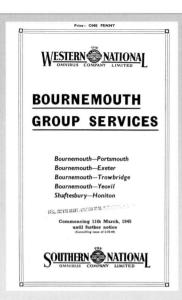

Price : ONE PENNY

WESTERN NATIONAL
OMNIBUS COMPANY LIMITED

BOURNEMOUTH
GROUP SERVICES

Bournemouth—Portsmouth
Bournemouth—Exeter
Bournemouth—Trowbridge
Bournemouth—Yeovil
Shaftesbury—Honiton

HULL, ESTATE AGENT, STATION ROAD,

Commencing 11th March, 1945
until further notice
(Cancelling issue of 1-10-44)

SOUTHERN NATIONAL
OMNIBUS COMPANY LIMITED

▲

Wartime restrictions brought express services nationally to a halt in November 1942. Royal Blue managed to keep ticking over with a handful of routes run as stage-carriage services. The coaches carried conductors armed with a ticket rack and 'part-fare' return tickets designed to be 'married' with those of a smaller value. This wartime 'Workman's Return' combination (journey forward to be completed by 9am), 2s (10p) plus 6d (2½p), was issued on Friday, at Stage 15 (Titchfield) on service 401. *Colin Morris collection*

▶

Postwar, there was a gradual reinstatement of express services — a process started in 1946. Until the 1948 summer season, the National companies were obliged to illustrate their albeit evocative Royal Blue timetable covers with the image in colour of one of their prewar 'standards' — still destined to soldier on for some time yet. Nevertheless, the picture captures that 'special' combination of sunshine roof and streamlined pannier. *Peter Delaney collection*

ROYAL BLUE
SERVICES

TIME TABLE

2D.

Commencing 13th October, 1947 until 9th May, 1948 (inclusive). Cancelling issue dated 19th May, 1947

The last 10 Bristol L coaches for Royal Blue were bodied by Duple. That firm also provided the bodywork for all 24 Bristol LL6B coaches divided equally between Western and Southern National. This was the longer (30ft) 37-seat version of the L-type, whose lines looked all the better for the extra length, producing — arguably — the most elegant Royal Blue of all. No 1275 (LTA 969), in the revised livery introduced in 1958, invites your opinion at Victoria. *Photobus*

If you're a politician, a poet or a 'pug',
    A turf commission agent or just a simple 'mug';
        If your Uncle Aloysius manages a Bank,
            Or your sister Angela is married to a Yank;
                If you just want to travel or have got to get around,
                    To see the sights and scenery or cover extra ground;
                        You'll find it more convenient and comfortable too
                            To go by Express Services run by Royal Blue.

The first Bristol LL6B/Duple coach, No 1250 (LTA 729) exits Bournemouth Coach Station in 1957 en route for Ilfracombe — and gives a good idea of the extreme care needed.
Colin Morris collection

oversee the running of the constituent bus companies on behalf of the British Transport Commission, to which the profits would now accrue. Thus Western and Southern National and, of course, Royal Blue were among the names which survived, their vehicle and operating policies retained in traditional Tilling style.

If anything, from 1952, Royal Blue went deeper into the Tilling-influenced fold, following the placing of contracts with Eastern Coach Works Ltd of Lowestoft (a Tilling-controlled company, as was the chassis manufacturer, Bristol) for all its subsequent coachwork during the next two decades. This coincided with the introduction to the fleet of the Bristol LS semi-integral coach, with six-cylinder Gardner engine beneath the chassis amidships, and with full-fronted bodywork.

The 'fifties continued to be a buoyant time, with national servicemen boosting weekend traffic as they made the most of their 48-hour leave passes. The Festival of Britain in 1951 and the Coronation celebrations in 1953 provided additional custom, which took advantage of increased night-time scheduling on several routes. Royal Blue coaches began to appear on service in new areas: the 1953 season saw the introduction of joint running with Maidstone & District Motor Services Ltd. From Totnes, Paignton and Torquay at the weekends, and from Bournemouth

◄ Designed in 1950, as a joint venture between Bristol and Eastern Coach Works (largely to eliminate the need to go outside the Tilling/BTC group for bodywork), the integrally-constructed Bristol LS, with engine amidships beneath the floor, represented the beginning of a new era in vehicle policy. For Royal Blue, the Gardner engine was selected, and No 1292 (MOD 979) was one of the first batch of 14, delivered with rounded glass quarterlights at the front, in 1952. *Photobus*

◄ On 3 June 1963, a telephone call from the Traffic Superintendent saw No 1279 (LTA 867) scurrying from the Rutland Road garage to Bournemouth Coach Station for use as a 'relief car'. Just two fitters are aboard, as this, the first of Royal Blue's Bristol LS6G coaches, passes beneath a canopy of trolleybus wires at Cemetery Junction. *Geoff Lumb*

all week, coaches of both companies ran via Hilsea and Hindhead to Maidstone, Gillingham and Chatham. There followed a joint venture with Southdown from Bournemouth via Petersfield to East Grinstead, and a joint service to the Isle of Wight, with Royal Blue coaches meeting the ferries of the Southampton & Isle of Wight Royal Mail Steam Packet Co Ltd (Red Funnel Steamers) at the Royal Pier, Southampton.

In June 1953, two Southern National Bedford OB small-capacity coaches were repainted in Royal Blue livery. Between 1955 and 1957, a further 64 Bedfords (one bodied by Thurgood and the rest by Duple) of the Western and Southern National fleets saw service in Royal Blue colours. These provided connections to and from minor resorts for passengers brought to exchange points by full-size express coaches, as well as doing local tours

work. Howard Evans (a Taunton-based inspector, eventually) started on such duties in 1956 at Bude, where Traffic Super-intendent Jack Gallagher told him: 'Ah! You can do the Royal Blue to Polzeath' (the feeder section for the London service, before handing over his passengers to the 'real' driver who would take the Bristol LS coach on to Victoria). When he was required to do the full 11hr 24min trip from Bude to London himself, he went 'flogging across to Okehampton, Exeter and up the A30 to Yeovil, Sherborne, Shaftesbury, Salisbury, Basingstoke and on into London — a hard road; long days!' Yet this was by no means the longest Royal Blue route.

Such was the weight of traffic on the main routes that many relief vehicles were hired, in addition to those 'borrowed' from Western and Southern National. First choice were the coaches

When the Bedford OB model was launched in 1939, Western and Southern National bought 19 of them — a process interrupted by World War 2. Deliveries recommenced in 1947. In the middle 'fifties, 66 of those which followed had their green areas of paint replaced by dark blue, and gained Royal Blue identities, for feeder and relief duties. No 1428 (LTA 904) of Southern National reminds us that these 27-seaters frequently went all the way to London.
Colin Billington collection

A degree of distracting light diffusion from the quarterlights caused a design adjustment at ECW, and Royal Blue's subsequent deliveries of Bristol LS6G coaches featured alterations to the front end — not least, for the drivers, a return to the opening windscreen. Resplendent in its original livery is No 1299 (OTT 98), one of 10 which arrived in 1953, pictured at Ribblehead on 10 August 1988 in the care of the Dorset Transport Circle.
Colin Billington collection

The rear end of an era. Carrying luggage upon the roof — a custom as old as the horse-drawn coach — was finally discontinued in the Royal Blue fleet with the withdrawal, in 1969, of the 1953 batch of Bristol LS6G coaches. For some 40 years, a luggage pannier and retractable chromium steps at the rear of the coach had been a familiar sight to following motorists.
Peter Delaney

A Bristol LS6G crosses the New Bridge at the head of Kingsbridge Creek, going westward on the route to Salcombe, Devon's most southerly Royal Blue destination, on the South Hams peninsula. This picture, which appeared upon Royal Blue timetable covers in the late 'fifties and early 'sixties, was probably one of Traffic Manager (Commercial) Clem Preece's publicity shots, taken at various points along his favourite road for such purposes, the A379.
Calton Phoenix collection

The big event in Bournemouth during the middle 'fifties was the considerable reconstruction of Hants & Dorset's bus station and the Royal Blue Coach Station beneath. Instead of going anti-clockwise around the central block, the coaches now entered down the old 'exit' ramp and progressed one-by-one in a southerly direction towards an exit in Pavilion Road, and up the slope into Exeter Road — a great improvement.
Ian Allan Library

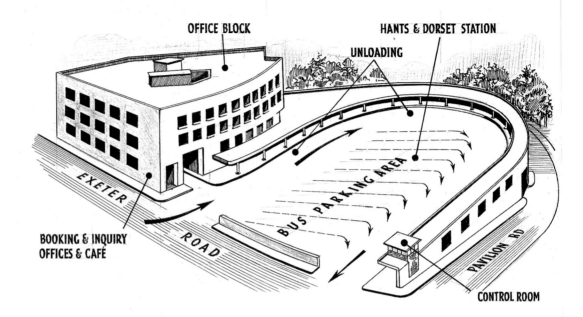

OFFICE BLOCK

HANTS & DORSET STATION

UNLOADING

EXETER ROAD

BOOKING & INQUIRY OFFICES & CAFÉ

BUS PARKING AREA

PAVILION RD

CONTROL ROOM

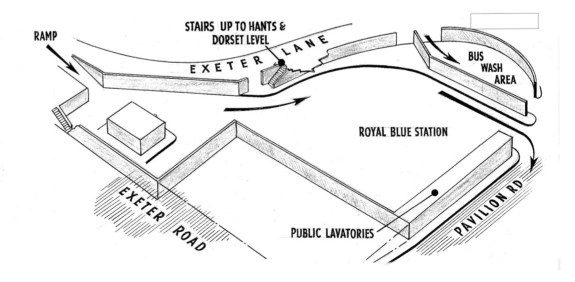

RAMP

STAIRS UP TO HANTS & DORSET LEVEL

EXETER LANE

BUS WASH AREA

ROYAL BLUE STATION

EXETER ROAD

PUBLIC LAVATORIES

PAVILION RD

In 1958 the Bristol LS was superseded by the MW (medium weight) model. Externally, the most noticeable difference was the provision of a radiator grille at the front. Twenty-seven MW6G coaches came into the fleet in 1958, 12 in 1960 and 16 in 1961. No 2258 (63 GUO), approaching Bournemouth Coach Station, having come up from the West Country, was one of the 1961 batch, and was nominally a Southern National vehicle. *Photobus*

of Hants & Dorset and Wilts & Dorset and nearby independents, such as Bere Regis & District and Princess-Summerbee of Southampton. Meanwhile, research as to where other visitors to the West Country were coming from led to an additional route being established in 1955, from High Wycombe via Salisbury.

In common with other operators, Royal Blue's fortunes suffered a double blow in 1956/7. First, in that winter, the Anglo-French conflict with Col Nasser's Egypt led to the return of fuel rationing; then, in July 1957, the operating staff became embroiled in a nationwide busmen's strike. Many journeys were lost accordingly.

On a brighter note, Royal Blue became a beneficiary of a 1953 decision by the Tilling Association to rebuild Bournemouth Bus & Coach Station. Designed by the Tilling group's architect, A. A. Briggs, the work was carried out over a two-year period commencing March 1957. The enlarged coach station beneath saw Royal Blue and other coaches enter down the old 'exit' ramp, but park in a much more spacious area situated below Hants & Dorset's service-bus area, and leave through a new exit at the rear. Even before work was complete, some 18,000 long-distance passengers per day were using the new facility, which also brought considerable relief to the parking problem at Rutland Road.

The reopening of the Coach Station followed the introduction of the Bristol MW (medium weight) coach and a new livery, all-cream above the waistrail. Sixty-six MW coaches were delivered between 1958 and 1963, the last 11 with restyled bodywork. Other examples were seconded to full Royal Blue service from the National companies. Following further amendments to the regulations governing vehicle dimensions, coaches of 36ft length entered the Royal Blue fleet from 1964 onwards and brought a seating capacity of 45 into service; the Bristol RE (rear-engined)

coach was also a considerably quieter vehicle than its predecessors. Forty-one REs with ECW bodywork were received up to 1970, labelled 'Royal Blue' from the ouset. However, by the end of the Tilling Association's administration, just 28 had entered the fleet. Again, RE numbers in the Royal Blue fleet were increased by vehicles brought in from Western and Southern National. Additionally, following the transfer to Western National of six ex-Silver Star Leylands in 1963, both National companies adopted a policy of painting all their coaches in Royal Blue livery (from their previous green and cream), but retaining their original company fleetnames — an idea which enhanced their suitability for use as express service relief vehicles.

The decade peaked in the 1965 season with an all-time record of over 1,556,000 passengers carried, but ended with a whipsaw of fortune: gains in traffic as a result of numerous branch railway-line closures, taken away to some extent by British Rail's electrification of the Waterloo-Southampton-Bournemouth line (a major competitor) in 1967; and the loss of the Bristol and Weston-super-Mare routes from Victoria upon transfer to the Bristol Omnibus Co Ltd in 1965, eased by new connecting services to Salisbury from Hitchin, Luton, Amersham and Slough. To these were added further joint routes to Stevenage, Southend and Norwich.

The winter of 1966/7 saw the abandonment of Royal Blue's long-standing 'A-Z' identification of its services. It now came into line with other operators and adopted an 'X' series of numbers which, for the first time, were displayed upon the vehicles; the Royal Blue network utilised X1-X32. The times were indeed a-changing!

Eleven MW coaches with stepped waistlines served long-term in the Royal Blue fleet, most of them in Southern National ownership. No 2271 (746 MDV) is one of the three which belonged to Western National. It has just left Bournemouth Coach Station, via Pavilion Road, on the South Coast Express service to Brighton, operated jointly with Southdown Motor Services Ltd; beyond Portsmouth, it would be officially 'on hire' to that firm. *Photobus*

Bristol's next technological advance was to produce a large-capacity, rear-engined vehicle — again in conjunction with ECW. This was the Bristol RE, introduced to the Royal Blue fleet in Gardner-engined form, as the Bristol RELH6G. No 2363 (ATA 105B) was a member of the first batch of 14 vehicles received in 1964. All those delivered up to 1970 provided seats for 45 passengers apiece. *Photobus*

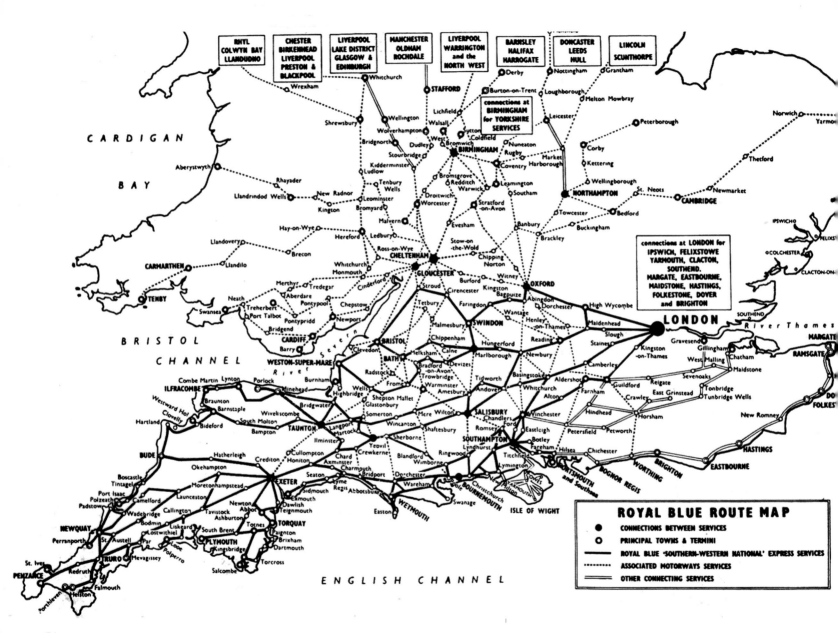

RHYL COLWYN BAY LLANDUDNO
CHESTER BIRKENHEAD LIVERPOOL PRESTON & BLACKPOOL
LIVERPOOL LAKE DISTRICT GLASGOW & EDINBURGH
MANCHESTER OLDHAM ROCHDALE
LIVERPOOL WARRINGTON and the NORTH WEST
BARNSLEY HALIFAX HARROGATE
DONCASTER LEEDS HULL
LINCOLN SCUNTHORPE

connections at **BIRMINGHAM** for **YORKSHIRE** SERVICES

connections at **LONDON** for **IPSWICH, FELIXSTOWE YARMOUTH, CLACTON, SOUTHEND. MARGATE, EASTBOURNE, MAIDSTONE, HASTINGS, FOLKESTONE, DOVER and BRIGHTON**

CARDIGAN BAY

BRISTOL CHANNEL

ENGLISH CHANNEL

ROYAL BLUE ROUTE MAP

● CONNECTIONS BETWEEN SERVICES
○ PRINCIPAL TOWNS & TERMINI
── ROYAL BLUE 'SOUTHERN-WESTERN NATIONAL' EXPRESS SERVICES
┄┄ ASSOCIATED MOTORWAYS SERVICES
══ OTHER CONNECTING SERVICES

5. NBC's Royal Blue

The Transport Act, 1968, which, among other things, brought the newly-nationalised BET bus interests and the still-recognisable Tilling-influenced area of the industry together again after a partition of some 26 years, led to the establishment of the National Bus Company with effect from 1 January 1969. The National Bus Company (NBC) should not be confused with the old National Omnibus & Transport Company or its subsidiaries, Western National and Southern National. The two latter had nurtured and greatly expanded the Royal Blue image. NBC's achievements would include its all-but-total erasure — old glory was destined simply to fade away over the next two decades. Another was to subsume Southern National under an overall Western National banner, which firm retained control over Royal Blue operations.

Administrative changes aside, there was not too much to show for the new regime. In a foretaste of what was to come, however, the NBC companies in the South West agreed upon a local area livery for coaches — white with an appropriately-coloured waistband. Those running upon designated Royal Blue routes had a dark blue band with white 'Royal Blue' fleetname. Two Daimler Roadliner coaches borrowed from Black & White had been used to evaluate this new Royal Blue livery. Bristol REs and later MWs were repainted into the new scheme, and new REs with Plaxton coachwork, and LH chassis with Duple, Plaxton and Marshall bodies followed between 1970 and 1973. Six AEC Reliance coaches with Willowbrook bodies to the narrower 7ft 6in specification, transferred from Devon General, also wore this livery and were used upon feeder services for routes to Bournemouth or London, etc.

Some six years later, the companies involved were to get together a marketing venture for London services from Bristol and the West Country, which they called 'Western Venturer'. With gathering momentum, NBC began to concern itself with a new corporate image to be used nationwide: stage-carriage buses would be either green or red, according to company, and uniforms, signs and stationery were to be standardised. NBC chairman Freddie Wood was convinced that most people found it difficult to differentiate between the various existing express coach liveries and those of the numerous independents pottering about on local private hire work. 'Some were unaware that an express coach network existed,' he said. Thus, in early 1972, the decision was taken to put all express services and extended-tour operations of the NBC subsidiaries under a new 'National Travel' banner. All National Travel coaches were to be painted white, with alternate red- and blue-lettered 'NATIONAL' logo. As a very small concession to those whose heart and soul were bound up in a traditional identity, the original fleetname was to be carried above the front wheel-arch, initially in small grey letters underlined with the appropriate colour. The latter refinement was soon supplanted by the fleetname only; and each and every one of those had to be in red. From now on, a Royal Blue coach would be white, with 'Royal Blue' in — red! Old habits die hard, however, and in everyday Western National administration, the staff still talked about the 'Royal Blue' services and organisation — so much so, that Jack Gleeson, the company's Area Traffic Superintendent based in Bournemouth, with specific responsibility for express operations, retained his title: TSRB (Traffic Superintendent, Royal Blue), and continued to do so until he retired in 1977.

In 1973, National Travel created geographically-separate operating companies. That of particular concern to the Royal Blue story was called National Travel (South West) Ltd. Its headquarters was in Black & White's home town of Cheltenham, with Ken Wellman as General Manager. Once again, however, the separate fleetnames (in red) survived. The operation of 'Royal Blue' services from Bournemouth was continued by Western National until May 1977, when control was assumed directly by National Travel (South West) — which continuation, happily, had enabled Inspector Jock Munro of the coach station and Tommy Gatrell at Rutland Road garage to collect their 40 years' service awards in March 1976. National Travel offered the Bournemouth Royal Blue drivers and clerical staff jobs at the Holdenhurst Road coach station of its subsidiary Shamrock & Rambler, and turned the Rutland Road garage into a coach maintenance centre, rather than an operating depot. It also promised what it termed 'an increased allocation of work elsewhere' for Royal Blue from its West Country depots. This was not yet the end for the Royal Blue name, but its long-standing association with Bournemouth was over. So too was that with Portsmouth and, more importantly, with London. National Travel (South West) Ltd acquired title to that sub-depot also, together with its ex-Royal Blue staff.

In July 1970, some 18 months after the formation of NBC, not much seems to have changed at Paris Street Coach station, Exeter; Royal Blue coaches (and a Black & White) are still in original livery. In the foreground is Bristol MW6G No 1436 (HDV 641E) of the Western National fleet. Since 1963, all Southern and Western National coaches had been painted in Royal Blue colours, so that they might be readily recognised whilst upon 'relief car' express workings. *Geoff Lumb*

Bristol RELH6G No 2379 (OTA 639G) was one of the existing coaches repainted into a new 'Royal Blue' southwestern area livery as NBC began to plan an overall image for itself. The vehicle is on transfer from Bournemouth Coach Station to Rutland Road, for servicing. It has arrived from London via Southampton and is passing the control room for Hants & Dorset's stage-carriage operations. *Photobus*

One of the last Royal Blue vehicles delivered with the old white-on-black registration plates, No 1301 (RDV 436H) of 1970 was a Bristol LH with Duple 41-seater coachwork. Since the waistband of the latter was comparatively deep, a rather generous area of dark blue was incorporated into its NBC southwestern area livery. Like this one, vehicles so painted operated tours as well as express services. *Photobus*

In early NBC dark blue and white livery on 7 April 1974 is Western National 1314 (UTT 580J), one of four Bristol LH coaches with Plaxton bodywork which entered the Royal Blue fleet in 1971. By the standards of the time, this 41-seater was a 'small-capacity' vehicle, its prime purpose being to provide a comparatively lightweight minor-road feeder service. *Colin Billington collection*

The third provider of bodywork for Bristol LH coaches in the Royal Blue fleet was Marshall of Cambridge (Engineering) Ltd. Ten of the type, delivered in 1973, were fitted with this uncompromising design as demonstrated at the builders by No 1316 (BDV 316L), the first of the batch. A total of 46 Bristol LH coaches wore 'Royal Blue' fleetnames, operating tours, feeder services, and express duties all the way to London. *Ian Allan Library*

New to Devon General, but transferred from the Green-slades subsidiary in 1970, No 1240 (937 GTA) was repainted by Western National into the new dark blue and white 'Royal Blue' livery. Just 7ft 6in wide, the coach is at Yeovil on a typical 'narrow-road' service; it was one of six such Royal Blue AEC Reliance 2MU3RV/ Willowbrook draftees which had been delivered new to neighbouring Devon General a decade before.
Peter Delaney collection

The early NBC 'regional' livery was soon replaced by the overall white imposed upon its subsidiaries' coaches nationwide. It did not sit too happily upon those older types repainted. No 2307 (974 WAE) was one such vehicle, but it had never worn dark blue, being instead one of 19 Bristol RELH6G/ECW coaches acquired secondhand from Bristol Omnibus Company in 1974. It is seen scurrying through Plymouth in August 1976. *John Robinson / Ian Allan Library*

The Leyland Leopard/Plaxton coach became an NBC standard: it looked good in its all-white livery. From 1975 to 1979, Western National took delivery of 74 examples which, at one time or another, wore red 'Royal Blue' fleetnames. No 2426 (GTA 807N) of 1975 exits Bournemouth Coach Station on a National Express departure for Aberdare, in what had previously been Associated Motorways territory. *Jenston Gwynne / Ian Allan Library*

Bristol RELH6G/Plaxton 47-seater No 2395 (UTT 564J) of 1971 in an early version of National coach livery — 'Royal Blue' appears over the front wheel-arch in grey with a bar of dark blue beneath to emphasise fleet origin. The vehicle is parked in the depths of Bournemouth Coach Station; a fire which started in the tyre store in the early hours of 24 July 1976, brought that famous landmark to a premature end. *Colin Billington collection*

In some ways a victim of its design concept, Bournemouth Coach Station (and Hants & Dorset's Bus Station above it) lies an abandoned ruin following the 1976 fire. The conflagration destroyed or severely damaged several Royal Blue and Hants & Dorset vehicles, and caused Royal Blue's Bournemouth terminus to be transferred immediately to Shamrock & Rambler's premises in Holdenhurst Road. The following May, the Royal Blue fleet withdrew to the West Country. *Philip Davies*

Just about as far west as it could go: delivered to Western National in white NBC livery with red 'Royal Blue' fleet-names in 1974, Bristol RELH6L No 2409 (PDV 409M), a 51-seater with Plaxton coachwork, rounds the snack-bar at Land's End (in the days before the location became a theme park), on a specially-provided tour duty. The vehicle was one of a batch of 17 fitted with Leyland engines. *Colin Billington collection*

During winter months, some Portsmouth-based Royal Blue drivers worked for Southdown, whilst other NBC subsidiaries 'borrowed' Royal Blue coaches for stage-carriage duties — Crosville and Alder Valley among them. Bristol MW6G No 1406 (744 MDV) was one of 14 loaned by Western National to London Country Bus Services Ltd in the winter of 1975/6. Based at Dunton Green garage, it is operating upon the latter's route 404 through Sevenoaks. *Peter Delaney collection*

No 3528 (AFJ 696T) was the first of ten 49-seat Willowbrook-bodied Leyland Leopard PSU3E/4R coaches delivered to Western National (in 1979, in this case). Amidst a veritable hive of Plaxton-bodied Leopards current at the time, they offered a welcome variation, despite being similarly dressed in the minimalist white livery of 'seventies National coaches. *Colin Billington collection*

Employing a great deal of imagination and an unexpected burst of sentimentality, the National Bus Company's executives decided to celebrate the 100th anniversary of Tom Elliott's start in the industry. At Dodington, seat of the Codrington family, wherein was a carriage museum, is No 3544 (FDV 800V), a brand-new Leyland Leopard PSU3E/4R/Plaxton 'bus grant' coach of Royal Blue, together with the carriage selected to participate. *Ian Allan Library*

Meanwhile, further Bristol RE and LH coaches joined the white 'Royal Blue' fleet, together with a growing number of Leyland Leopard coaches with Plaxton bodywork, which — with small ongoing modifications — became NBC's standard coach for several years. With the addition of further new and second-hand examples (some with Willowbrook bodies), by 1980 over 90 Leopards had, at one time or another, carried the (red) Royal Blue fleetname in Western National Omnibus Co ownership. So too did four others of earlier vintage, borrowed from Southdown for the 1973 summer season, and three Bedford YRT coaches transferred from Greenslades to Western National and used from 1978-80.

When Western National lost its 42-year-old Bournemouth residency in 1977, it retreated westward in what would be called in military parlance 'good order'. It did not surrender its Royal Blue vehicles to National Travel (South West) Ltd, but retired to the West Country with them, where they were reallocated to various Western National depots. The promised increased allocation of work materialised — bits of old Royal Blue and Associated Motorways routes and other duties elsewhere — so that there were 'Royal Blue'-labelled coaches working to places they would not otherwise have visited. Most of the Western National depots had their own Royal Blue drivers and, as Traffic Manager Michael Rourke recalls, '… they were on the whole promoted to Royal Blue from the bus staff — and this was a career move, really… You were a member of the élite if you

The Royal Blue 'centenary' gathering in 1980 brought together NBC Chairman Lord Shepherd (and Lady Shepherd); senior officers of NBC and Western National, a hired four-horse coach and several preserved Royal Blue coaches for a celebratory run between Holmsley and Bournemouth. Fine; but 1880 was the year Thomas Elliott got his first licence to drive a cab. His first replica 'stage coach' was licensed in April 1894. Thomas and his wife Elizabeth are not on record as having claimed anything to the contrary (see text). *Michael Rourke*

En route from Holmsley to Bournemouth is the lightly-disguised coach hired by NBC for the Royal Blue 'centenary'! Built by Shanks in the 1870s as the 'Defiance', it had been operated by Tilling at Hampton Court between 1937 and 1939 as the 'Coronation Magnet'. Brought to Holmsley from Dodington specially for the event, in the care of Colin Henderson, the coach sported a lick of newly-applied blue and red paint to complete a very pleasant illusion. *Michael Rourke*

Out of a suitably sepia-toned past comes preserved Bristol LL6B/Duple coach No 1269 (LTA 898), participating in the 1980 'centenary' celebrations with a run, as of old, from Exeter. It was originally delivered in May 1951 to Southern National, with which it served the express routes for 13 years. Ted Cox, the driver who originally brought it new to Bournemouth, drove it once again in 1980. *Colin Billington collection*

The classic lines of Terry Durrant's and Brian Traves' preserved Bristol LL6B No 1269 (LTA 898) grace the courtyard of the Cat & Fiddle Inn, Hinton Admiral, in May 1980. When the vehicle was new in 1951, its roof also would have been dark blue. The inn was a most appropriate place to stop; in horse-carriage days, Tom Elliott kept a change-team stabled there. *Michael Rourke*

On 28 August 1983, Trathen's Volvo B10M No 66 (BDV 866Y) leaves London for Plymouth via Gloucester Road (near Earl's Court), in which road a parking lot had provided that operator with a terminus prior to its gaining access to Victoria Coach Station. As part of the joint operation launched the previous year, the vehicle also bears red 'Royal Blue' fleetnames.
Colin Billington collection

went on to Royal Blue from a Western National garage… You had to earn your spurs a bit.'

An interesting flurry commencing in 1982 was an NBC-sponsored co-operative venture between Western National and the Plymouth-based private operator F. G. Trathen & Sons — following a period when the latter had run in competition with National Express — marketed under the new buzz-word 'Rapide'. Gone were the days when express-coach passengers actually liked cruising through villages and beautiful countryside to get, eventually, to their destination. The new generation of customers wanted to get there as quickly as possible, and along the motorways, of course. 'Trathen's Skyliner — West Country-London Rapide' vehicles were impressive three-axle, double-deck coaches, with hostesses serving refreshments, and with video and toilet (now removed, airline-fashion, from the proximity of the otherwise-engaged passengers). For its part, Western National was obliged initially to provide ageing Leopard coaches for the service until the autumn of that year. Then, five new (single-deck) Dennis Falcon coaches with Duple Super Goldliner coachwork upgraded the NBC contribution somewhat. Both Trathen's and Royal Blue travelled from Plymouth to London via the M5 and M4 — more new territory for Royal Blue.

By now, the National Bus Company was, for Margaret Thatcher's Conservative Government, an unwanted legacy of socialism. Ordered to prepare itself for its own demise, NBC set about dividing up its operating subsidiaries into saleable packages, prior to a forthcoming privatisation of the industry. In 1983, 'Western National' was retained for Cornwall, Plymouth and the West Devon area, 'Devon General' was revived in what was basically its predecessor's old area centred on Exeter, 'Southern National' was revived for Dorset and the previously Western National area of Somerset, and a completely new name — 'North Devon', trading as 'Red Bus' — was chosen for the North Devon area. Each received a share of white Royal Blue coaches. Devon General, Southern National and North Devon chose to replace the Royal Blue fleetnames on these with their own (in red, of course). In contrast, the new 'Western National Ltd' decided to retain the Royal Blue title on its coaches operating out of Plymouth and Cornwall on National Express operations. Says Michael Rourke: 'Whether they were given the right, or Managing Director David Rabey took it upon himself, I do not know.' Either way, it kept the name alive just a little bit longer.

Western National provided seven new Leyland Tiger (single-deck) coaches — five with Plaxton bodies, two with Duple — for the joint Royal Blue/Trathen's Rapide service, introducing them over a two-year period between 1983 and 1985. During the summer of 1984, however, it supplemented these with eight three-axle MCW Metroliner double-deck integral coaches in National Express livery — some of which carried 'Royal Blue' fleetnames. In 1986 it was decided that this practice would be discontinued; by 1988, the name had disappeared from coaches still in service.

That, however, is not entirely the end of the story. The new, and now privatised, Southern National company, based at Taunton, took the decision in 1992 to have a surviving Bristol RE/ECW coach restored to full blue and cream Royal Blue livery. This vehicle it proceeded to run on its remaining local express routes, such as the Exeter-Taunton-Bristol run. The biggest stir was caused by its appearance on the X94 service — Bridgwater-Taunton-Bournemouth — the last coach in Royal Blue livery to operate a revenue-earning, scheduled express service, and a 'proper' Royal Blue putting in an appearance in the home town of the founder. This grand and nostalgic gesture made, Southern National finally withdrew the vehicle from service in June 1994.

Safe in the care of several dedicated enthusiasts, a selection of post-World War 2 Royal Blue coaches survives, from those in early stages of restoration to some in fully-refurbished running order. The famous dark blue livery chosen in the 19th century by Thomas Elliott has been faithfully resurrected. Back in Bournemouth, however, it is perhaps Henry Laidlaw's ghost which enjoys the last laugh. The fleetnames 'Royal Blue', 'Tantivy', 'Rover', 'Shamrock' and 'Rambler' are all no more. Only 'Excelsior' remains alive and well — and in Holdenhurst Road, too. He'd better not laugh too heartily though, because the founder of that firm (c1923), Walter Maitland, rode an Excelsior motorcycle and rather liked the name. There was no other connection.

People generally tend to remember the originators of a famous trading name, rather than the identity of those who choose to get rid of it, which, as the authors of *1066 and all that* would have said, is a 'Good Thing'. However, as a cautionary note, I conclude with an anecdote from Michael Rourke. When the title 'Southern National', rather than 'Western National', was about to be restored in 1983, he went to Weymouth to unfold the glad tidings to the local citizenry. 'Well,' came the reply, 'us didn't really notice it had been changed in the first place.'

In 1982, Western National took delivery of five Dennis Falcon coaches with Duple 47-seat bodywork, expressly for services upon the 'Rapide' operation from Devon to London. All initially bore 'Royal Blue' fleetnames, but No 2351 (AOD 644Y), about to depart for Exeter, was subsequently re-flagged with the 'Greenslades' subsidiary title, since it was based at Torquay rather than Plymouth.

Colin Billington collection

▲ A rather expansive version of the 'Venetian blind' style of livery incorporated a generous amount of the original Royal Blue colour. At Southampton, amid Bristol VRs and Leyland Fleetlines of the Hampshire Bus fleet, is No 2206 (A530 WRL), a new Leyland Tiger TRCTL11/3R with 46-seat Plaxton Paramount coachwork, delivered in 1984. It was later repainted in National Express 'Rapide' livery. *Solentslide*

No 2222 (B337 BGL) was one of a pair of Leyland Tigers delivered to Western National in 1985 with 46-seat Duple bodywork. It entered service with this National Express 'Rapide' livery in order to supplement the company's double-decker coaches which entered service the previous year. The vehicle is being 'shunted' at Victoria Coach Station on 31 August 1985. *Colin Billington collection*

About to depart on service 500 from Victoria to Plymouth, No 1404 (A759 VAF) was delivered to Western National in May 1984, dressed in National Express 'Rapide' livery with Royal Blue fleetnames. It was one of eight MCW Metroliner DR130 integral coaches, the first four of which carried the traditional name until Western National decided to dispense with it. *Colin Billington collection*

▲ The Royal Blue fleetname still survived on 5 April 1988, despite a 1986 announcement by Western National that its use would be discontinued. Plymouth-based 'Cornwall' coach No 2438 (LOD 728P), a Leyland Leopard PSU3C/4R with Plaxton body, is seen at Camborne en route to Penzance. Its original white livery has been replaced by the traditional dark blue, and chevrons of 1920s charabanc sky blue.
Colin Billington collection

▲ With screen set for the most distant location to appear upon a
Royal Blue express coach, Western National's Leyland Leopard
PSU3C/4R/Plaxton 49-seater No 3500 (KTT 808P) of 1975 waits
at Plymouth on 23 May 1986. Built to bus grant specification
— with folding doors — the vehicle wears a latter day NBC
'Venetian blind' livery. *Colin Billington collection*

▲ One of five Leyland Tiger TRCTL11/3R coaches with Plaxton bodywork, No 2208 (A532 WRL) was received in May 1984 with 'Royal Blue' fleetnames. On 6 April 1985, at Victoria, however, awaiting the long run to Penzance, it instead carries Western National's 'Cornwall Coachways' local identity as it contributes to the 'Rapide' service. *Colin Billington collection*

It fell to Southern National to claim the honour of running the last coach in service with full traditional Royal Blue livery. Long since converted to dual-purpose configuration, 1970-vintage Bristol RELH6G/ECW coach No 1468 (RDV 419H) was nearing the end of its 'second life' at Taunton on 14 May 1994. It had besported itself from that town upon both stage-carriage and express work.
Colin Billington collection

Further Reading

Among the books I have found helpful and/or recommend for further reading are: *The Years Between 1909-1969 Vol 3: The Story of Western National and Southern National from 1929* by R. J. Crawley and F. D. Simpson (Calton Promotions, 1990) — amazingly well researched and written, and quite the best transport company history I've read; *History of Royal Blue Express Services* by R. C. Anderson and G. Frankis (David & Charles, 1970), for its very detailed accounts of traffic court proceedings and Royal Blue operations under Western and Southern National control;

History of Hants & Dorset Motor Services Ltd (the proper title) by Colin Morris (David & Charles, 1973) and *Hants & Dorset — a history* (the proper title) by Colin Morris (DTS Publishing, 1996), both for information about Royal Blue and Tourist tours and excursions under that company; *Victoria Coach Station: the First Fifty Years 1932-82* by Frank Woodworth (Victoria Coach Station Ltd, 1982); and *Wheels to the West* by Clem Preece (Travel & Transport Ltd, 1974); also numerous articles over the years in *Buses Illustrated* and *Buses*, journals published by Ian Allan Ltd.

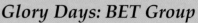